Orphans of the Storm

About the Author

John R. Walker is a freelance foreign affairs columnist for a number of Canadian newspapers.

He was foreign affairs analyst for Southam News, a news agency for 17 Southam newspapers across Canada, and travelled widely in Third World countries, reporting and writing a column on world affairs. Prior to that, he headed Southam bureaus in Washington, London, Ottawa, Tokyo, and Beijing.

He won a National Newspaper Award in 1983 for his coverage inside Afghanistan. In 1986, he was appointed a Fellow with the Canadian Institute for International Peace and Security, writing, among other things a background paper on "Canadian Press Coverage of Arms Control and Disarmament Issues." In 1989, the North-South Institute published his survey, "Third World News Coverage" in Canada.

Orphans of the Storm

PEACEBUILDING FOR CHILDREN OF WAR

John R. Walker

between the lines

© John R. Walker, 1993

Published by:

Between The Lines
394 Euclid Avenue, #203
Toronto, Ontario
M6G 2S9

Cover design: Goodness Graphics, Toronto
Cover photograph: UNICEF/Roger Lemoyne
Interior design: Goodness Graphics
Typesetting: Moveable Type, Toronto
Printed in Canada

Between The Lines gratefully acknowledges financial assistance from the Canada Council, the Department of Communications, the Ontario Arts Council, and the Ontario Ministry of Culture, Tourism, and Recreation, through the Ontario Publishing Centre.

All rights reserved. No part of this publication may be reproduced, stored in a retrieval system, or transmitted in any form or by any means, electronic, mechanical, photocopying, recording, or otherwise, except as may be expressly permitted in writing by the publisher.

Canadian Cataloguing in Publication Data

Walker, John R., 1920-
 Orphans of the Storm: peacebuilding for children of war

Includes bibliographical references.
ISBN 0-921284-78-0 (bound) ISBN 0-921284-79-9 (pbk.)

1. Children and war. 2. Orphans. 3. United Nations – Armed forces. I. Title.

HQ784.W3W3 1993   362.7'3   C93-094099-7

CONTENTS

Preface		Page 7
Introduction:	The Children of War	9
Part One:	Youth: The First Victims	13
	The Problem of War	17
	An Era of New Opportunities	23
Part Two:	Cease-fires: Some Success Stories	31
	El Salvador	35
	Lebanon	44
	The Sudan	51
	Iraq, Iran, and Kuwait	60
Part Three:	War-torn World: The Troubled Search for Peace	69
	Horn of Africa: Ethiopia/Eritrea	73
	Horn of Africa: Somalia	79
	Mozambique	89
	Sri Lanka	98
	Burma/Myanmar	106
	The Philippines	114
	Colombia	122
	Yugoslavia	129
Part Four:	Growing Up Peaceful: A New International Consensus.	137
	The Limits of Sovereignty	141
	The Right to Help	153
	Corridors of Tranquillity	163
	Building Blocks of Peace	168
Part Five:	Peacebuilding for Children: A Manifesto	177
Endnotes		187
Bibliography		191

The author would like to acknowledge the support of the people at the Centre for Days of Peace, and especially the advice and editorial assistance of Penny and Clyde Sanger.

PREFACE

In November 1991, the **Conference on Humanitarian Ceasefires: Peacebuilding for Children** was convened in Ottawa, Canada. It was sponsored by the Centre for Days of Peace, Ottawa, and co-hosted by Canadian Physicians for the Prevention of Nuclear War, the Canadian Public Health Association, and UNICEF Canada.

The Centre for Days of Peace is a non-partisan association of groups and individuals working to promote the idea of "days of peace" — negotiated humanitarian cease-fires with the goal of bringing aid to civilians in zones of conflict, and if possible providing opportunities for building peace. It acts as a catalyst, encouraging international organizations to make this concept a priority.

The 100 conference participants came from 23 countries, including 12 conflict zones, to discuss, to network, and to provide insights about an urgently important subject whose successes, possibilities, and limits had never been reviewed before at an international conference. The dynamics of this conference were fascinating and encouraging. In some cases, people from countries engaged in civil war were meeting together for the first time, discussing their problems face to face, and for their sake the conference was closed to the media. The atmosphere warmed up rapidly and the sessions were frank and useful — more so, as one experienced aid official put it, than discussions on these subjects at the United Nations or at the usual international conferences.

This book is not simply a conference report but the author's examination and expansion of the ideas and proposals raised at this unusual session. By spreading the message about helping children and other civilians in war zones, perhaps this book will do its part to encourage conflict resolution and promote the peace process, and thereby build on the ideas raised and the work done at this unique meeting of minds.

■ *Introduction*

THE CHILDREN OF WAR

Ali Reza took the holy "wine of Imam" and went into battle when he was barely 11, a potential martyr for Islam. At 12, a veteran Iranian soldier in his khaki fatigues, he sat, curly black hair thick over his sober brown eyes, on his green rug in the barracks of the Ramadi prisoner-of-war camp in Iraq, minus his left foot.

A black-robed mullah in his hometown of Shafh persuaded this small child to join the Baseej, Iran's volunteer force of young and old that supported the army and the Revolutionary Guards in their sacred war against Iraq. He was part of a "human wave" attack that led the tanks across the minefields against Iraqi positions in the Basra area. But this time, the protection of his God, Allah, failed. An Iraqi shell took his foot, and he was abandoned by his Iranian colleagues on the field of battle.

Fifty pairs of eyes watched and fifty pairs of ears listened as he recounted his sad tale, trying to be brave and not denounce his country before his fellow prisoners. But quietly, with downcast eyes, he admitted that what he missed most was his mother and father. He desperately wanted to go home. He did not then know that he would have to remain in that barren camp for another six years.

~ ~ ~

On a sunny, fall day, they came up the dusty valley to the little Afghan tea-house, slowly, painfully, dejectedly. The father, in his baggy brown *shalwar kameez* and dirty sweater, was leading the overburdened donkey, while mother followed bearing a sack on her shoulders. Sitting on top of the family's meagre possessions on the animal's back was a small, pale-faced, frightened girl.

Her name was Siddiqa and she was eight. Her right arm was bandaged where a hand had been. Her father said they had abandoned their bombed-out house near the besieged Khost valley in Paktia province after MIG fighters strafed their village. Food became very scarce because corn and grain fields had to be left unharvested. And then their daughter had been wounded picking up a brightly coloured plastic stone; it was in fact a mine. Soviet helicopters had dropped some of these deadly missiles on a road leading past their house.

Siddiqa lolled listlessly on the donkey, unsmiling and unwilling to talk. The family trudged on, with a day's walk to the Pakistan border ahead of them, hoping for a hospital bed for Siddiqa. Her war was nearly over, but not her trauma, nor her years in a dusty refugee camp.

౼ ౼ ౼

Ernesto had flashing black eyes, unruly dark hair, and was sullenly wise for his 10 years. Ragged, barefoot, he sat with his mother on a low wall inside a Catholic refugee camp in El Salvador one hot, spring day.

She recounted how they had been forced to flee their village in the hills north of the capital when the Salvadoran army made a sweep through their region. Along with some other men, Ernesto's father had been picked up, marched to the edge of the village and shot in full view of the family. Now they were refugees inside their own country. "We are still in great danger," the mother said. One of their neighbours in the village had left the camp recently to go to mass in a nearby church, was picked up by armed civilians, and never seen again.

■ INTRODUCTION ■

Apparently unfazed by what he had been through, young Ernesto said proudly, "My father was a revolutionary." And would he support the revolution? "Yes," he exclaimed with moody fervour, while his mother attempted to shush him. He had become uncontrollable since his father's death, she said. Civil war seemed to have hardened him at a tender age and he was trying to bury fear and grief with bravado.

His war would last until he grew to manhood, unless, like so many, he escaped to the hills to fight and die as a child warrior with the guerrillas.

೧ ೧ ೧

Three children, the author remembers, among hundreds of thousands, whose impressionable, growing years were spent in countries where war had become the normal focus of life and a vicious school for children.

Part One

YOUTH:
The First Victims

Children, as we all know or often proclaim, are the future. War is a failure of the past looming over that future. In the early 1980s, Nils Thedin, head of Sweden's delegation to the UNICEF executive board, began to think about children as the world's most innocent, vulnerable, and dependent citizens, especially in wartime. He began speaking of "children as a zone of peace," thus recognizing their special needs and their unique claim on the attention of the world during times of crisis or war. The underlying intention of this concept has inspired many actions—among them, "days of tranquillity" to vaccinate and provide humanitarian services for children and their families in zones of armed conflict, and "corridors of peace" to bring aid to families in war-torn regions.

THE PROBLEM OF WAR

The twentieth century has the unenviable record for being the most warlike in history. In this era, man's inhumanity to man, largely demonstrated through military strength, makes Europe's Hundred Years' War seem almost like a tournament of chivalry.

It is the adults of our societies, with their ideologies and their cravings for power, their aggressiveness and their follies, who start wars. It is the young men, and nowadays young women, who must fight them. And it is the young children who suffer the most from death and injury, and the maiming of their lives psychologically before they have even begun to experience the wonders of existence.

There may be, of course, just causes for wars where people are driven by years of social or economic injustice to rebel. There are wars of desperation that involve the very survival of a people, a race, or a tribe, where the desperate priority is merely to keep the victims alive so their heritage remains. But a war fought for a just cause is no less devastating in its effects on its victims. Without children, there is no future on this planet, no heritage, and the global picture of what faces the world's children, and their families, is a tragic one.

Casualties

"So far, in the 90 years of this century, there have been over four times as many war deaths as in the 400 years preceding," according to the latest edition of Ruth Leger Sivard's annual survey of world military expenditures. Wars now are shockingly more deadly and destructive, and civilians, principally women and children, are the major targets. "In this century many more unarmed civilians than professional soldiers have died in war. In the decade of the 1980s, the proportion of civilian deaths jumped to 74 per cent of the total and in 1990 it appears to be close to 90 per cent."[1] And that was before the Gulf War, the Kurdish and Shiite revolts in Iraq, and the civil war in the former Yugoslavia.

Since 1945, following the two world wars that led the century in bloodshed and destruction, there have been, according to the United Nations, an estimated 20 million people, the majority of them women and children, killed in more than 182 armed conflicts. Civil wars and ethnic conflicts in more than 30 countries have also created a new category of refugee, "internally displaced persons." These refugees in their own homelands, mostly in Africa and Asia, number more than 20 million, a total that exceeds the number of international refugees, estimated at just over 18 million. As a result, children have had the most vital years of their youth disrupted, the basic requirements of their education and health lost, and their human rights ignored. Today's wars are also more dangerous for children because, with so many civil conflicts where there are no front lines, where fighting is so fluid and nasty, it is almost impossible to avoid military action and very difficult to halt it by political negotiations.

Leah Levin of the British Human Rights Network writes: "Children are deprived of the protection of parents and family; they are exposed to brutality and atrocities which leave them scarred for a lifetime. Frightening evidence of the torture and slaughter of parents in the presence of their children, and of the torture and mass killing of children, in counter-insurgency action by military forces in a number of countries, has been carefully documented by human rights organizations."[2] And it is happening in every war zone.

In the destruction and chaos of war, the lives of children are threatened by disease and starvation as well. As was seen in Ethiopia and the Sudan, food and its distribution are used as weapons of war and politics. Food-aid convoys have been attacked and halted, or medical and food centres destroyed, causing the deaths of thousands of women and children.

While the end of the Cold War and the growing demands of

peoples for more democratic institutions has happily reduced a number of the major wars around the globe, there are still some 20 countries in which major armed conflict continues to rage and perhaps 20 more where ethnic violence is growing. The Stockholm International Peace Research Institute defines a major conflict as "a prolonged combat between the military forces of two or more governments, or of one government and organized armed opposition forces, involving the use of manufactured weapons and incurring battle-related deaths of at least 1,000 persons." But, of course, during insurgencies many of the deaths are not incurred in battle but in terrorist raids, under torture, and during the indiscriminate destruction of homes.

The lives and health of children are still at stake in the terrorized countryside of Angola and Liberia, in the war-torn chaos of Somalia, in the ravaged hills of Guatemala and Peru, in the Kurdish mountains of Iraq, in the deserts of the Sudan, in the jungles of Sri Lanka, Burma (Myanmar), and the Philippines, as well as in the urban jungles of bombed-out Yugoslav towns. The horrors of war, so fleetingly experienced by well-fed Westerners on nightly colour TV news shows, are etched in the minds and faces of the victims, especially the young children.

The Effects on Children

Depending on their upbringing, there can be an amazing degree of resilience among the young, despite the scream of bombs, the rattle of automatic weapons, the fiery destruction of homes and buildings. As Anna Freud pointed out in her book *War and Children*, about the London Blitz: "War acquires comparatively little significance for children so long as it only threatens their lives, disturbs their material comfort, or cuts their food rations. It becomes enormously significant the moment it breaks up family life and uproots the first emotional attachments of the child within the family group."[3]

That report, cited in *Unaccompanied Children*, a mid-1980s study that confirmed the trauma children suffer by separation from their families in more recent wars like that in Vietnam, was written long before the latest arsenal of modern weapons came into use. Now children of the intifada have learned that Israeli "rubber" bullets can kill and maim because they are 95 per cent metal pellets covered with a thin rubber coating. The children of Afghanistan have found even pretty plastic toys can be mined. We are only beginning to learn the devastating effects of smart bombs, cruise missiles, cluster bombs, and fuel-air explosives on the children of Iraq, who have already, courtesy of their own regime, faced the silent terror of chemical warfare.

When war becomes "normal life" and terrifying experiences are routinely suffered, young children may begin to experience what doctors call "chronic post-traumatic stress disorder," as has happened with many of the children who survived the genocidal war years in Pol Pot's Cambodia. They relive their brutal memories in nightmares, they become hypersensitive to any reminder of it, or they are troubled by guilt for surviving their murdered parents or siblings.

On the other hand, children at play learn how to cope in the adult world and often tend to imitate it. In the West Bank refugee camps, children play as Palestinian demonstrators against those playing Israeli soldiers, beating with sticks, firing home-made guns, or pretend gas canisters. Outside those camps, some 50,000 children have been wounded in the real world of the occupied zones of Israel. In Northern Ireland, the kids in the street use the IRA as a role model for their "wars" against the British army, thus imitating their parents' views. Later they can taunt the foreign soldier in real life and join the catcalling between Catholic and Protestant that keeps the strife and killing going in Belfast and elsewhere.

The War Machine

Although United Nations protocols for war insist that no children under 15 years of age can be engaged as soldiers, it is a tragic fact of modern warfare that thousands of boys as young as 10 have been impressed into Third World armies, as in Iran, Uganda, and Liberia, or swept by revolutionary enthusiasm into guerrilla armies, as in El Salvador or Peru. The world's varied war machines grind on, even after the post-Gulf War euphoria about cutting back on arms, and those machines inevitably require new recruits as much as new military equipment. A new arms race is now blossoming. The Gulf War was barely over when the United States sold Saudi Arabia $14-billion worth of its new high-tech weaponry, and deals for billions more in the Middle East have been completed. By 1992, even the disintegrated Soviet Union was into a fire-sale of its weaponry, legally or illegally.

Many UN studies have shown that defence expenditures have an adverse effect on a nation's health care. It is most appallingly evident among poor Third World countries, where health and education expenditures go down as military ones go up. A 1986 World Bank report showed that the 43 countries with the highest infant mortality rates (over 100 deaths per 1,000 live births) spent three times as much on defence as on health. As it says in a recent study, *No Place To Be A Child: Growing Up in a War Zone*, looking at war-scarred children reminds us that "some of the worst consequences of today's wars are not physical and psychological, but social. Wars produce social dislocation, of which one consequence is a breakdown in the basic 'infrastructure of life.' All too often this includes food, health care and education."[4] It also results in a sorry life for children in squalid refugee camps, urban slums, or barracks for orphans.

In the book, *Peacemaking in the 1990s*, Dr. Joanna Santa Barbara, a Canadian psychiatry professor and president of Canadian Physicians for the Prevention of Nuclear War, writes: "In many cases ... poverty exists alongside the wealth of a national elite and is held in place by the oppressive might of the government's army. Very often the government is the army and frequently the 'stability' of this situation is supported by military aid and intervention by a superpower. When people, oppressed beyond endurance, arise in protest, the army strikes back and the country is at war. This dynamic underlies many of the wars currently killing children with bombs and bullets, while more children die of malnutrition and disease held in place by the war system."[5]

It is this inhuman, indiscriminate warfare, wreaking havoc on the lives, health, and psychological well-being of all civilians, but especially children, that has to be dealt with now and for the future.

Children are made adults before their time by war largely because adults have failed to prevent the conflicts that engulf them both. As Elie Wiesel, himself a "child of war," has said: "More than anything—more than hatred and torture—more than pain—do I fear the world's indifference."

AN ERA OF NEW OPPORTUNITIES

According to James Grant, the dynamic executive director of the United Nations Children's Fund, "a new humanitarian order" has been established in the world during the last three years, and children will be the main beneficiaries.

The UNICEF chief was talking specifically about the recent UN Convention on the Rights of the Child, which was adopted by the General Assembly in 1989 and came into force on September 2, 1990, and about the World Summit for Children held at the United Nations in September 1990. But he was also referring to the recently successful efforts to promote humanitarian cease-fires in war zones in order to provide medical attention and food aid to children and families in dire need of such help.

In addition to its mention in the Universal Declaration of Human Rights, there had been, since 1959, a specific UN declaration on the rights of the child, but it was not binding on states. The objective of the new convention, which took about ten years to negotiate, was to make it a legal responsibility. As Grant said at the Ottawa conference, it is "the first global codification of the rights of every child, and of the legal obligations of society and adults to protect those rights." He has called it "the manifesto of a new ethic for children, shared by nations throughout the world." The convention's 54 articles cover the rights of children in war and peace, their rights to health care and education, their protection from exploitation and abuse, and their general survival. From then on, it was laid down, the welfare of children should have "first call" on the global society's concerns and capacities, whether in times of conflict or of peace. A ten-nation committee was established to investigate and publicize violations of those rights.

The World Summit for Children, on the other hand, was

designed to take action for the protection and development of children around the globe. Held at the United Nations, it was the largest gathering of world leaders in history, with 71 heads of state and 88 senior ministers in attendance. In their public commitment, they pledged among other things to "work carefully to protect children from the scourge of war." In order to accomplish such high-minded undertakings, they set out a "Plan of Action" with specific targets. These included such general subjects as child health, nutrition, the role of women and the family, education and literacy, and protection from exploitation and poverty. It set a target: to reduce infant and under-five child mortality rates in all countries by one-third between 1990 and the year 2000. In its article on "protecting children during armed conflicts," it took special note of an idea that had been successfully acted upon in the previous five years. That was the example of suspending hostilities to allow for "days of peace" to vaccinate children or creating "zones of tranquillity" to aid mothers and children in areas of war.

The revolutionary world in which we live has set the stage for changes more far-reaching than could have been envisioned even three years ago. As UNICEF's annual report records, "In 1990 the international climate had undergone dizzying, unexpected changes in the direction of freedom and cooperation. Bold advances wrought by perestroika in the Soviet Union, the transformation of Eastern Europe and subsequent reunification of Germany all contributed decisively to the end of the Cold War that had divided East and West and militarized the world economy. There were hopes for an early redirection of military funds towards social spending."[6] Military dictators were replaced by democrats in Latin America, and by 1991 one-man rule was under attack in Africa, and apartheid was being dismantled in South Africa.

New ideas were springing to life in the global institutions as they had not done since the end of the Second World War. "Since wars begin in the minds of men, it is in the minds of men that the defence of peace must be constructed," as it says in the constitution of UNESCO.

Early Efforts Towards Peace

When thinking people, after the sufferings of two world wars, formed the United Nations in 1945, they dedicated it to saving succeeding generations from the scourge of war, to reaffirming faith in fundamental human rights, to establishing conditions for respecting international law and justice, and to promoting social progress and better standards of life for all. Its agencies, like UNICEF, the UN High Commissioner for Refugees, the UN Special Fund, the World Food Programme, and the UN Disarmament Commission were devoted to helping children, refugees, and less developed peoples and sought to disarm an over-militarized world.

Yet for the first 40 years of its existence, the United Nations was hampered as a collective-security organization by the ideological battles and armed conflicts created by the Cold War between the United States and the Soviet Union. And this prolonged struggle, under the expanding cloud of the nuclear threat, hampered in many ways the operations of the UN agencies devoted to helping children, stopping wars, and aiding the developing world. Even UN peacekeeping forces, devised to help staunch the flow of blood, did not encourage much peacemaking because of this ideological confrontation.

To fill the gap, to take humanitarian action where huge international agencies could not go, a flood of non-governmental organizations (NGOs) sprang up, private aid agencies that could work at the grassroots level, especially in Third World countries, with more flexibility and local awareness than large international bureaucracies. NGO work, both foreign and domestic, in dozens of countries, has become a vital complement to the aid efforts of governments and the United Nations, and to the peace work of the UN and the International Committee of the Red Cross.

Help for Children

For a long time, workers in the field, both from the UN and NGOs, worried about the fate of children in war-torn countries where they distributed aid and worked on projects of development. Providing health care, and aiding the injured or the homeless, was often difficult, even impossible in war zones. One of these people was Nils Thedin, head of Sweden's delegation to the UNICEF executive board. He began in the early 1980s to argue passionately in UN circles about his idea of "children as a zone of peace." Children, he declared, obviously represent our future and should be given protection in time of war. Wherever possible, provision of aid to children could be facilitated by a temporary halt to hostilities or by ensuring safe passage through battle zones. Furthermore, the cooperation and negotiation needed to save children might help the larger peace process itself. By aiding and protecting children, we adults might encourage the work of conflict resolution, might be able to bring peace from war.

But UN agencies are limited in their ability to act in conflict areas. Almost all armed conflicts today occur between a government and a national opposition movement and thus are considered, by the UN Charter, as internal matters; UN involvement would thus constitute an affront to national sovereignty. Unless the government involved allows international scrutiny, UN action on the issue is very difficult and often obstructed.

James Grant took the Thedin idea a long step further. Over lunch one day in July 1984 with President Napoleon Duarte of El Salvador, he raised the subject of the 20,000 Salvadoran children who were dying each year during the civil war, largely from diseases that could be prevented with a 50-cent shot of vaccine per child. There were more casualties from disease than from the war, he argued. Why not call a halt to the war to immunize all the children on both sides? El Salvador's "days of tranquillity" for a vaccination campaign was the result.

The El Salvador campaign became part of a global UN vaccination campaign aimed especially at Third World countries, where vaccine-preventable diseases were claiming nearly five million children's lives annually and leaving millions crippled. As a result of this program, pursued throughout the world, the yearly total of death by disease among children was cut in half by the end of 1990 and is continuing. But while the immunization rate in many Third World countries was climbing to nearly 75 per cent in the late 1980s, in those with ongoing wars the rate could be as low as 15 per cent in the conflict areas.

Grant's idea of cease-fires for inoculations began slowly to spread, but there was no existing organization with the freedom, focus, and resources to promote "days of tranquillity" in the many other war zones of the world. It was in this spirit of filling a gap, of pushing a humanitarian activity that international organizations might be reluctant to grasp, that a group of non-governmental activists in Canada's capital began to think about a rather grandiose but appealing idea that they called "Five Days of Peace" — to vaccinate the children in all the world's war zones.

Dr. Edward Ragan, program director of the Canadian Public Health Association's international immunization program, was intrigued by the success of the children's immunization campaign in El Salvador, which he'd heard of by chance from UNICEF sources. As he said in an interview, "Why didn't I know about it in 1985, when I was involved in the world immunization program?" (Probably, it might be said, because there was so little media coverage of it in Canada.) "So I wondered, why couldn't there be 'days of tranquillity' in other war zones? I talked to Murray Thomson, chairperson of Peacefund Canada, and said, Wouldn't it be a great idea if we could form a small group to generate interest in such "days of peace." We decided five days would be needed for this immunization work. Since I was on the board of the Canadian Physicians Against Nuclear War, I decided to talk to Randy Weekes, the executive director, and it captured his imagination too. We soon formed a group of about 18 and began discussing ways to organize such a program."[7]

Dr. Ragan, meanwhile, had been sounding out leading health officials at the 1988 World Health Assembly and the Canadian Council of Churches, all of whom were enthusiastic. And a League of Red Cross/Red Crescent official told him that the organization was planning a "World Campaign for the Protection of Victims of War" in 1991 that would involve a two-day truce for such activities as immunization.

The Five Days of Peace committee toiled on, networking, researching war zones, and securing funding from the Canadian International Institute for Peace and Security (CIIPS) for a paper on humanitarian cease-fires. It struggled with the question of whether to get its feet wet in a particular conflict or to remain in the background trying to spread ideas and experience. It eventually opted for the latter. Meanwhile, the high-profile Red Cross campaign had to be reduced to a concert for peace and some research papers, after that organization found how complicated it was to set such cease-fires in motion.

Dr. Ragan and the Canadian Public Health Association encouraged the Canadian government to take a stand for continuing immunization as a priority at the 1990 Children's Summit. The Five Days of Peace group at the same time was asking Prime Minister Brian Mulroney, who was to be co-chairman of the summit, to include an item in the UN Summit "Plan of Action" that would identify the success of humanitarian cease-fires and the further need for them to help children in war. Dr. Ragan said that Yves Fortier, Canada's ambassador to the UN, went to bat for it and talked with the Swedes, who eventually proposed Article 25 in the summit "Plan of Action." "There is no question we did make a small contribution to the appearance of that article," he said.

"Days of tranquillity" and "corridors of peace" were by then being used with varying success in Lebanon and the Sudan. The

Children's Summit declaration, signed by leaders of 156 countries, says in Article 25 of its Plan of Action:

> *Children need special protection in situations of armed conflict. Recent examples in which countries and opposition factions have agreed to suspend hostilities and adopt special measures such as "corridors of peace" to allow relief supplies to reach women and children and "days of tranquillity" to vaccinate and to provide other health services for children and their families in areas of conflict need to be applied in all situations.*
>
> *Resolution of a conflict need not be a prerequisite for measures explicitly to protect children and their families to ensure their continuing access to food, medical care and basic services, to deal with trauma resulting from violence and to exempt them from other direct consequences of violence and hostilities.*
>
> *To build the foundation for a peaceful world where violence and war will cease to be acceptable means for settling disputes and conflicts, children's education should inculcate the values of peace, tolerance, understanding and dialogue.*[8]

The need for some kind of humanitarian cease-fires to help children and their families in war situations has now been recognized at the highest level. But there is no sure way to enforce all the statutes. Aroused public opinion and global censure may help, along with education, yet civil wars, ethnic conflicts, and religious struggles are often extremely hard to halt.

Besides, as Robin Hay says in his CIIPS paper:

> *There are no pat definitions of humanitarian cease-fires. They are usually arranged on an ad hoc basis when a humanitarian need in a war zone becomes or has the obvious potential of becoming particularly acute.*
>
> *The need, whether it be child immunization to raise immunization levels in the conflict zone and prevent a mass epidemic, or*

food delivery to prevent mass starvation, tends to override the immediate military-strategic interests of the conflicting parties. It becomes what is known as a superordinate goal: a goal about which it is in the mutual interest of the combatants to cooperate, and the fulfillment of which detracts from neither their military nor their political/strategic position.

Humanitarian cease-fires are distinct from traditional cease-fires in that they are not arranged for the express purpose of creating time for the disputants, or the disputants plus a mediator, to negotiate terms of a conflict resolution. In this sense, they are fundamentally humanitarian in origin, not political. Neither are they conceptualized in the same way in which traditional cease-fires are conceived: The organizing feature may be primarily time (five days of peace), space (corridors of tranquillity), or both (corridors of tranquillity lasting for a fixed period of time).[9]

Ed Ragan and his colleagues in what soon became the Centre for Days of Peace, believed that pushing the concept of "days" or "corridors" or "zones of peace" could also help in the process of conflict resolution, of reaching for real peace. So from the minds of these Canadians, with the support of humanitarian figures abroad, came this Conference on Humanitarian Cease-fires: Peacebuilding for Children. It was a first effort to spur some discussion and action on Article 25 of the Summit for Children.

■ *Part Two*

CEASE-FIRES:
Some Success Stories

"This is the story of the 17 camels. The story is set in a village, in a country far away. The custom in this village is that a person's worth is measured by how many camels he or she owns. There was a man living in this village who owned 17 camels. He was old and died. He had three children and his estate was to be divided among them, leaving one-half of the estate to his oldest child, one-third to the middle child, and one-ninth to his last child. Unfortunately, 17 camels cannot be divided by these fractions, so the children began to squabble over the division of their father's wealth.

"Now, in this village there was a tradition of consulting elders of the community when trouble arose. So the children took their dispute to a wise old woman of the village. She listened to their dilemma, thought about it, and decided the answer to their problem was for her to give them her only camel. Now their estate consisted of 18 camels, and the estate could be easily divided, as the father wished. The oldest child got 9 camels (one-half of the estate), the middle child got 6 camels (one-third of the estate) and the last child received 2 camels (one-ninth of the estate). Now you may note that 9+6+2=17. So the wise old woman took her 18th camel and went home.

"The moral of this story is that sometimes people can be so caught up with a conflict they fail to find a fresh perspective and often need an outsider to do this for them."

—as retold by Dayle Spencer, director of the conflict resolution program at the Carter Center, Atlanta, Georgia.

EL SALVADOR

The smallest, most densely populated country in Latin America is, ironically, named "the Saviour." But tiny El Salvador has, for more than a decade, been having disastrous trouble saving itself.

The peace accord and treaty between the government and the opposition forces, brokered by the United Nations on the last day of 1991, has ended the prolonged civil war that devastated El Salvador. But it is the background to that brutal, often sadistic war that can explain the need for, and the success of, a unique series of humanitarian cease-fires—pauses in the war that saved thousands of children's lives and may have helped in the long process of peace negotiations.

The Historical Background

For nearly a century, El Salvador, lying along the balmy Pacific coast of Central America, has been run by an oligarchy of land-owning families. These so-called "Fourteen Families" used much of the arable land for tobacco plantations, later expanding to cotton and sugar, while the poor peasants who worked the fields were landless, undernourished, and increasingly restless. The rich families found they badly needed the army during a 1932 peasant uprising led by Augustin Farabundo Marti. Allegedly to keep order, the army slaughtered some 30,000 peasants. The oligarchs later decided to share power with the army, and from 1948 until 1979 a series of military men graced the presidential palace in San Salvador while the wealthy land-owners gave the orders. The U.S. government, which became concerned about left-wing revolution in the Third World and the rise of Fidel Castro, began in the 1960s to provide military training for its Latin American friends, especially the Salvadoran rulers. It was all counter-insurgency training to keep restless peasants in line.

When a group of reformist junior officers took power in a coup in 1979, their junta, which included civilians, promised an end to military corruption and a major land-reform program. The latter was designed to counter the attractions of peasant guerrillas under left-wing leaders, who had been fighting in the hills for some years to end the rule of the land-owners. These rebels became known as the Farabundo Marti National Liberation Front (FMLN).

When the reform movement collapsed in 1980, the FMLN declared all-out war. A former popular democratic leader, Napoleon Duarte, returned from exile and was pressed into the leadership by the military and the Americans, then confirmed as president in a 1984 election. El Salvador became a pawn in President Ronald Reagan's obsessive fight against communism in Nicaragua and elsewhere in Central America. As a result, the country sank into the morass of an ugly civil war, in which brutal methods were used by both sides. The peasants saw the destruction of their villages, the murder of their leaders, and the suffering of their children, while the well-to-do plantation owners retired to luxurious safety in Miami.

The "Days of Tranquillity"

In the midst of this turmoil, in 1984, UNICEF director James Grant had his historic luncheon with Duarte in New York City. The concept of "children as a zone of peace" had been percolating in his mind for a while, and the idea that for a mere 50 cents each you might be able to save some of those Salvadoran children who were dying from preventable disease in this tiny nation impelled him to speak out to President Duarte.

Grant knew that the World Health Organization had started a global immunization plan. In developing countries, as few as 5 per cent of the children were immunized against common fatal diseases. The United Nations was gearing up in 1984 to boost by 1990 the number of children vaccinated world-wide against the six most common contagious diseases: diphtheria, whooping cough, tuberculosis, tetanus, measles, and polio.

The persuasive Grant reminded President Duarte of the political benefits should such a campaign be successfully completed in his country within the length of one presidential term. The Salvadoran president was convinced but doubted that the FMLN guerrillas would allow vaccination teams in their areas. Besides, it would be too dangerous.

Then, Grant rejoined, what about getting a temporary cease-fire? He insisted UNICEF would only vaccinate children on both sides in the war. Both sides would have to agree. In El Salvador, that meant both the government's very independent military forces and the various guerrilla forces of the FMLN coalition.

With Duarte's acceptance, the next step was to undertake a feasibility study. UNICEF and the Ministry of Health in El Salvador conducted the study, along with the Pan American Health Organization. The latter agency had launched a seven-point plan that year called "Health: A Bridge for Peace in all of Central America" that included a vaccination program for children. The plan of action that UNICEF now proposed called for three national immunization days a year for the next three years.

The Salvadoran government had to find a way to negotiate a cease-fire with the FMLN and it was not an easy task. The Salvadoran military feared any humanitarian cease-fire would imply recognition of the FMLN and its aims. Duarte and his health officials were reluctant to negotiate with the guerrillas themselves. A mediator was needed, and in Catholic El Salvador who better than the Catholic church, with its network of priests all around the country and its solid record for defending human rights? Three Catholic leaders—Archbishop Arturo Y Rivera, Monsignor Rivera Y Damas, and Monsignor Rosa Chavez — were chosen to contact the guerrillas and keep in touch with the government.

Negotiations began, and the FMLN leaders told the church team they were interested. Vaccinations would be of great importance to their people, living as they often did in the mountains or the jungle under constant army harassment or attack. Talks proceeded by indirection. The Ministry of Health would propose areas for immunization around the country to UNICEF officials, who would then pass them on to the church team. Its members would in turn communicate them to the guerrillas, who, having made modifications or alterations, would return them via the same mediating channels. And it worked, as Robin Hay sums it up in his study on the subject:

> The end result of this non-negotiation was a non-cease-fire: an unsigned agreement in which each group agreed not to promote armed activities on the days of the immunization campaign if the other would do the same. Great care was taken by UNICEF not to refer to the agreement as a truce or a cease-fire but as a period or day of tranquillity.

The agreement was tentative until the last moment. Then at eight o'clock on Sunday morning of February 3, 1985, after the firing had ceased, the first day of vaccination began. Dr. Hector Silva, a medical doctor and president of the Commission for Social Welfare of the Salvadoran National Assembly, told the Ottawa conference, "The first time was the most difficult." It had helped, he said, that "Duarte was publicly involved in advocating the program," that pressure from abroad, especially the United States, and even from the Pope, had persuaded the Salvadoran army to go along, and that the FMLN recognized the "good public relations" they would gain by their agreement. He noted that the three days chosen for 1985 were all Sundays so that the religious leaders, both Catholic and Protestant, could preach to their flocks about the urgency of having their children vaccinated. Positive publicity of all kinds was an "essential aspect" of such humanitarian cease-fires, he said. The newspapers played up the campaign and there were almost 12,000 spot ads on radio and TV. About a million leaflets were distributed, sometimes by air over FMLN regions, along with brochures and posters.

There were 1,800 vaccination sites located around the country for this first-shot blitz. Although UNICEF and the Red Cross had a major role, along with the government health authorities, in running the show, many other organizations contributed, including the Rotarians, the Lions Club, and the Boy Scouts, in getting people to the centres in cities. But as Dr. Silva said, in El Salvador "you have to go to different military posts, you have to deal with different warring organizations within the FMLN itself. And NGOs on the ground know and relate to all the local situations and how the different organizations will react." While the NGOs were important in getting medicines through, the church, he said, had a crucial role because it knew and understood best the political and cultural background against which the whole operation was taking place.

As Dr. Silva observed, winning the hearts and minds of the people is crucial in such an operation. "Community participation makes a difference," he said. He recalled how, in 1984, the Americans had tried to win all hearts by suddenly sending into villages a health-care team, "with a clown, candy, a dentist, a couple of nurses to look at 150 patients, even some beer." But it was all a public relations manoeuvre. The "days of tranquillity" were different, since local leaders, local priests, and known NGOs were all involved and inspired public trust.

After that first Sunday, the vaccination days became almost "automatic." The army, which had initially been most reluctant to co-operate, felt the pressure from the United States, while the FMLN was concerned for the welfare of the people and for their new recognition in the negotiation process. The outside world was amazed to see pictures of an FMLN fighter with an assault rifle slung over her back inoculating a Salvadoran baby sitting on another guerrilla's knee while a government nurse worked nearby.

By the third year, the health authorities in San Salvador reported that cases of polio and tetanus had dropped by about two-thirds and cases of measles, a major cause of child mortality, had dropped by 80 per cent. Mark Schneider, senior policy adviser to the Pan

American Health Organization, reported that the "days of tranquillity" have continued with success every year up to the present and have reached some 300,000 children a year. In 1990 there was not one case of polio in El Salvador. He cited these statistics of inoculations: In 1985 anti-TB shots given to 49 per cent of the children, in 1990 to 60 per cent; diphtheria shots to 55 per cent of the children in 1985, to 76 per cent in 1990; polio shots to 54 per cent of the children in 1985, to 76 per cent in 1990; and measles shots to 54 per cent of the children in 1985, and to 76 per cent in 1990.

Humanizing War

The Salvadoran government also had to deal with migrations caused by the civil war. Twenty-five per cent of its population fled to Honduras and elsewhere abroad and 25 per cent became "internally displaced," usually in church refugee camps. As the political atmosphere changed between 1987 and 1991, many of these people were repatriated to their villages, located in military belts. Humanitarian cease-fires, negotiated by local NGOs, were needed to allow people to move from one area to another for food and medicine.

Later, the problem of helping the wounded and handicapped of the FMLN came up, and the International Committee of the Red Cross undertook lengthy negotiations with a reluctant army to get casualties to Cuba and Mexico for medical attention. A similar agonizing negotiation, this time through the UN High Commissioner for Refugees, was necessary to allow these recovered men to return to El Salvador. The army's concern on both occasions was strategic, not humanitarian. As Dr. Silva observed, the army was not as afraid of the vaccination campaign, since there was no military advantage to the enemy in it, whereas the removal of the wounded to hospitals was seen as a possible help to the FMLN. If left with the guerrillas, they would slow them down, but if returned to them they could be healthy fighting men again.

As a result of the Salvadoran operations, the Pan American Health Organization now endorses the principle, according to Mark Schneider, that "humanitarian cease-fires should be institutionalized wherever and whenever there are conflicts." Several lessons were learned from the efforts in El Salvador to "humanize war." First: "a humanitarian purpose — vaccinating children — could not be halted by either side." Second: the importance of universality — "the beneficiaries of the national immunization campaign were all the children of El Salvador, none were excluded." Third: "the benefits could not be diverted for use by either side for partisan benefit." Fourth: "the international guarantors of impartiality in the conduct of the humanitarian cease-fire are from UNICEF, International Committee of the Red Cross (ICRC), UN and the Organization of American States (OAS)," well-recognized agencies. Finally: "there were no easy opportunities to enhance either side's military position, so none could benefit militarily," Schneider concluded.

In the seminar on El Salvador at the Ottawa conference, the participants found some other lessons as well. First, they thought it was important that a government that tended to ignore their advice had been forced to deal with non-governmental organizations, both foreign and local. Second, they noted that, as a result of the process of negotiation and action, support had been given to building the internal infrastructure for health services, and that the local communities became more aware of their rights to food and medical care. And also the process had forced political discussions to be moved from behind closed doors in the cabinet and military headquarters and into open, public debate.

Peacebuilding

But what effect did these negotiations for humanitarian cease-fires — and they had to be undertaken each year — have on the political problem of reaching a peace settlement in El Salvador? Mark

Schneider feels that "to a certain degree, the humanitarian cease-fires did offer an opportunity for a new channel of dialogue to occur, however tenuous, between not only the FMLN, its interlocutors, and the high command, but in some instances also the local military commanders, and that clearly is of even greater consequence."

Dr. Silva is convinced that the process brings actors of a more moderate tendency into negotiations, and that the continued practice in establishing these cease-fires is helpful for the future. When there was difficulty over repatriating guerrillas from their hospitalization in Cuba, contacts between some of the negotiators helped the final successful agreement. The seminar group was even more positive, arguing that "after seven years' experience, it can be seen that the process of humanitarian cease-fires has had a reinforcing effect on the peacemaking dialogue."

Julia Devin of the International Commission on Medical Neutrality, an independent group which monitored violations of the right to health care in Salvadoran war zones, said a humanitarian cease-fire is one method of pushing this right forward. It is also one of the many links in the peacebuilding process. She pointed out how her commission had exerted pressure on the Salvadoran government as the conflict escalated in 1989 by involving the U.S. Congress in urging recognition of those rights to health care that had been ignored in the war. The Salvadoran government was persuaded to issue a declaration in 1990 publicly recognizing the Geneva Conventions and health-care rights, which the Medical Neutrality Commission then got the FMLN to accept. As larger UN negotiations for peace were under way at that time, the commission turned over its material on these issues to be included in the humanitarian agenda of the UN talks.

After 18 months, those talks, under urgent pressure from retiring UN Secretary-General Javier Pérez de Cuellar, came to a successful conclusion on December 31, 1991, ending 13 years of civil war that had cost the lives of some 75,000 people, the majority of them women and children. After the accord was signed, Dr. Silva observed that "peace became viable because the U.S. wanted it. They were spending too much money here. They were spending it because of fear of Communism and Communism is no longer here to fear." It could also be added that the demise of Soviet Communism had its effect on Cuban and Nicaraguan aid to the FMLN and helped to modify its political and economic program. Neither side could win the war, and the global pressure from the UN, combined with all these varied factors, produced the peace treaty signed in Mexico City on January 16, 1992. The next twelve months saw El Salvador slowly work its way back to civil life.

LEBANON

Lebanon was once one of the Mediterranean's most prosperous and attractive trading centres, and Beirut, its capital city, was something of a rich and decadent Paris of the Middle East. For millions of people living in the televised 1970s and 1980s, however, Lebanon brings to mind only car-bomb attacks, shelling of bullet-scarred modern buildings, indistinguishable militia armies forever fighting each other, and troops from Israel, the United States, and Syria intervening.

Lebanon is a small country that has suffered through civil wars for the last 16 years. But it has to be understood that this is the result of its being an artificial nation created by imperial powers, a nation whose chaotic existence has been further complicated by the impact of the Arab-Israeli conflict.

The Historical Background

By secret agreement during World War I, later sanctioned by the League of Nations, France obtained a mandate over Syria, and Britain a mandate over Palestine. The French carved Lebanon out of Syria in 1920 and the country was given its independence in 1943.

Although Maronite Catholics were originally the dominant people in the Lebanese mountain country, Sunni and Shiite Muslims prevailed in the rest of the country. Lebanon's original constitution laid down that its president should be a Maronite, its prime minister a Sunni, and the speaker of the parliament a Shiite. It was a recipe for religious antagonism, cultural divisions, and weak government. Or, as David Gilmour writes in *Lebanon: The Fractured Country*, it was "a country with no unity, a country without a sense of nationalism, and a country whose citizens were not loyal to the state but to their religious communities."[1] And more recently, it might be said, to the power of their secular militias.

Palestinians were first added to this unstable mix when they came as refugees fleeing from Israel, newly created in the 1948 war.

More came following the Six-Day War of 1967 and again when driven out of Jordan in 1970, until there were some 350,000 of them in a population of 2.5 million, living wretchedly in 17 refugee camps, many near Beirut.

As was perhaps inevitable, in 1975 the administrative control of Lebanon broke down completely. In Beirut—where the rich lived splendidly in high-rise apartments and villas in the hills while the poor seethed in the fetid slums, the place where Christian West met Muslim East—the civil war began with a massacre. Gunmen from the major right-wing Maronite party, the Phalangists, ambushed a bus party of Palestinians. The majority of Lebanese did not want war; it was unleashed by extremist factions, militia bosses fighting for turf. As government collapsed and the army sided with the Maronites, all attempts at cease-fires failed. The barricades went up, the shutters came down, the snipers took up position, the fighting raged, the arms trade blossomed, and the war spread around the country.

Syria finally intervened in 1976, fearing the country might break up and Israel might move in. The Arab League negotiated a peace, but it didn't last. Violence continued, and in 1978 Israel attacked southern Lebanon to clear out Palestine Liberation Organization (PLO) "terrorists" and establish its own Lebanese puppet force along the border. Israel's major invasion came in 1982 to drive the PLO out of Lebanon. It laid siege to Beirut, bombing and shelling a modern city of 1.5 million with suction bombs, cluster bombs, and phosphorus shells. In the first two weeks of that invasion, some 14,000 people were killed and 20,000 wounded, mostly women and children. In the Sabra and Shatila refugee camps for Palestinians, Israeli forces looked on as Phalangist militiamen massacred some 2,000 men, women, and children. This prompted an ill-fated, short-lived multinational peacekeeping force of U.S. Marines, French, British, and Italian troops to enter Beirut to restore order. The car-bombing of their barracks soon drove them out.

There was a short-lived cease-fire but there had been 180 cease-fires between 1975 and 1983 and none had ended the war or allowed for much humanitarian aid. So the fighting continued until Israel withdrew in 1985. Meanwhile Syria had begun meddling in Lebanese affairs again, this time encouraging the Shiite Amal militia to attack the Palestinian refugee camps to drive out the radical Palestinian militia. This resulted in the brutal "war of the camps" in 1986-87.

Dr. Chris Giannou, a Canadian surgeon who worked in the Shatila camp for 27 months, told the conference how foreign intervention and misunderstanding played a major part in the Lebanese conflict. He described how the Syrian-inspired siege of the camps had frustrated humanitarian cease-fires and prolonged civil war.

> *I was in the Palestinian camp of Shatila. It is 200 metres by 200 metres with a population of 3,500 people, entirely surrounded by an enemy militia. The battle broke out in November 1986, and six months later we were still under siege and still being bombed. After six months there was not much left in terms of food and medical supplies in the camp. The shantytown-type dwellings of the camp had received over 250,000 shells, tank, mortar, and heavy artillery. And the hospital in the middle of the camp had itself been targeted specifically.*
>
> *There were several attempts to have the United Nations Relief and Works Agency (UNRWA) bring in convoys, with the UN flag flying, of food and medical supplies. The negotiations went on for the cease-fire over several hours to allow the trucks access to the camp. There was a price to pay for every truck that came into the camp: a similar truck with relief supplies to be given to the enemy militia. The first three convoys managed to reach the camp, and before we could unload the food, the lorry trucks were hit by a rocket-propelled grenade and all the food supplies went up in flames before our eyes. Ultimately, a cease-fire was imposed for non-humanitarian reasons. Political reasons.*

Political pressure at the UN and in the Arab League brought Syrian troops back in to enforce cease-fires in Beirut, even around the camps. So the blockade of food and medicines was lifted, although the Shiite Amal siege continued until January 1988.

Humanitarian Cease-fire

The continual flow of televised news about conditions all over Lebanon, plus reports from his local agents, inspired UNICEF's James Grant in 1986 to see what could be done at least about immunizing children. It took nearly a year of negotiating for Grant and UNICEF's Middle East regional head, Richard Reid, to get an agreement with all the parties in a chaotic country where there was no obvious mediator in sight.

Finally the Lebanese authorities were persuaded to follow the Salvadoran example and agree to a humanitarian cease-fire in order to vaccinate the country's children in the fall of 1987. There were many areas outside Beirut where no vaccinations had taken place during the past 12 years of civil war. Dr. Giannou had already managed to vaccinate in his bomb shelter all 800 children under 12 in Shatila three times.

Since the government did not control many regions, and since Christian and Muslim factions were often at each other's throats, Grant and Reid needed to contact the interested parties, whether Maronite Phalangists, Shiite Amal, Muslim Druzes, pro-Iranian Hezbollah, or even the Syrians and Israelis. They explained that, because of this neglect, infant mortality rates were way up and there was danger of epidemics. They noted that children's diseases were causing between 1,000 and 2,000 deaths and several thousand cases of blindness or crippling every year among Lebanese children under five years of age.

UNICEF finally got its agreement. There would be a cease-fire for three days, beginning on September 23, to be followed by one each in October and November. A campaign was launched to inform the public through radio, television, and the newspapers. Armed militiamen distributed leaflets telling mothers to have their babies vaccinated. Mullahs spread the word in their mosques.

Before the deadline, roadblocks were lifted to allow UNICEF trucks with medical equipment and vaccines, as well as government nurses and ICRC personnel, through the various check-points to 29 districts of Lebanon. When the shooting ceased, vaccinations were held in 762 medical centres, largely without incident. Sometimes UNICEF people did have minor problems. The telephone system was unreliable and gas for some vehicles unavailable. But here the fighting men helped with their own efficient communication and transportation systems.

As Khatmeh Osseiran-Hanna, executive director of Save Lebanon, a charitable organization working with children, told the conference: "UNICEF was even able to use [Lebanese] militiamen to deliver aid. They got militiamen to put pharmaceuticals on tanks and deliver them to villages all over Lebanon." Hardly a symbol of peace, she added, but that's how it worked. She said that there was one problem: the so-called "security belt" in southern Lebanon. "UN Security Council Resolution 425 asks specifically for the withdrawal of Israelis from there and it has not been implemented. In that area there are no NGOs, no UNICEF, that have been able to reach people ..."

Although there was no inoculation in the border belt, the main vaccination campaign had to be extended a fourth day. The booster-shot days, scheduled for October and November, were held when fighting had already died down in most areas of the country.

The Lebanese civil war intensified in 1989-90. Some areas of the country that had been previously untouched by the conflict were devastated. In Beirut during the summer of 1989, only 200,000 people out of its 1.5 million inhabitants remained. Eventually, as Iraq's invasion of Kuwait in 1990 won the world's attention, Syrian troops intervened again, and with outside pressure, the guns were finally silenced in December. A pro-Syrian coalition government of National Reconciliation was formed that ordered the withdrawal of all the militias to a position outside the 1000-square kilometre area of Beirut and its suburbs. Since then, a new government, elected despite a Christian boycott, has been attempting to assert its control over and rebuild the entire country. But it still faces political factionalism, corruption, and the legacy of 16 years of war—a war that left 150,000 dead, some 700,000 wounded, and nearly 40,000 handicapped, out of a population now over 3 million. About 1 million people were displaced by the devastation, 80 per cent of them permanently. Among families, 89 per cent found diseases more frequent than before the war, 27 per cent reported malnutrition, 24 per cent of the children were not attending school, and 45 per cent of the children were traumatized by their experiences.

The local representative of Save Lebanon, Dr. Amal Shamma, who lived in Beirut throughout the civil war, reported on the effect of this chaotic war on children:

> Killing and injury have not only been objects of fear and anxiety for children in Lebanon, but also of fascination and play. One study has revealed that over 80 per cent of children speak of the war, a fact corroborated by parents and teachers, and that one-third prefer war toys to any other toys.
>
> In streets, children are seen to enact the scenes of killing, kidnapping, and torture that they have heard of or actually witnessed. After outbreaks of shelling or a car bomb, children rush to the streets to witness rescue efforts and collect souvenirs. Conversations with children may reveal a great emotional detachment in their detailed description of scenes of death.
>
> Children have been seen in and around hospital emergency rooms helping transport the injured or carrying pieces of human bodies to the morgue. In hospital rooms, the most common toy of children admitted for war-related injuries is a toy gun, an M-16 or

AK-47, or for the luckier ones, a complete toy army. An injured, fantasizing child may describe injuries suffered during random shelling as occurring "while he fought the enemy and tore him to pieces."

Teachers who have been interviewed about the behaviour of their students, in addition to noting the symptoms of fear, anxiety, and depression, also note that war and war activities are an important part of their pupils' conversations, play, and drawings. Increased aggressiveness and rebelliousness were a common finding.

And many crossed the boundary between imagination and reality, joined their brother's militia, and fought in the real war, she added.

Ms. Osseiran-Hanna suggested to the conference that peace-building "doesn't have to wait until people are exhausted by war. Children can be helped by peace education" to learn that conflict is not the only way to solve these problems. Clarence Shubert, a senior adviser for UNICEF, showed the conference a film on how education for peace was promoted in Lebanon. In 1989, building on the idea of humanitarian cease-fires and "children as a zone of peace," a magazine called *Sala* was started. Its articles discussed the culture of the various peoples of Lebanon and of the need for respect and justice for all. Letters came in from some 40,000 young people in response. The magazine's proponents organized summer camps where Muslims, Christians, and Druzes lived together, played together, worked together, and learned to respect each other's points of view, cultures, and religions. By using educational activities, dance, and art, these camps were said to help the children to get to know each other so they could, in Shubert's words, become "agents of peace." He said about three-quarters of Lebanon's young people had undergone peace training in these camps by the end of 1991.

THE SUDAN

The land of ancient Nubia, now the Sudan, is the largest and one of the poorest countries in Africa. A majority of Arabic-speaking Muslims inhabit the largely desert lands of the northern provinces, while black Africans of animist or Christian beliefs live mostly in the semi-tropical savannas of the south. In nearly six decades of the Anglo-Egyptian Condominium that governed the Sudan until its independence in 1956, there was little development in the pastoral, farming, and swampland regions of the south. But there was one change: some successful efforts to Christianize the black population. At the same time the Arabic north began to prosper economically.

Historical Background

Sudanese independence was born in conflict as the people of the south sought to end economic discrimination by the government in Khartoum and obtain equality of treatment. A military coup in 1958 exacerbated the situation when the new leaders started the "Arabization" of the African provinces and expelled the Christian missionaries. A nasty 17-year war began, though it was generally ignored by the world press. It was brought to an end in 1972 by General Jaafar Muhammed el Nimeiri after he seized power in another coup. He granted a form of autonomy to the south: religious freedom and its own local parliament in a capital at Juba.

Nimeiri's efforts at administrative decentralization in the early 1980s were complicated by an army mutiny in the south and a new movement for southern autonomy. He had abrogated provisions of the 1972 peace accord and, under pressure from fundamentalist Muslims, had made Islamic *sharia* law, a strictly Muslim set of laws governing all aspects of human activity, applicable to the whole country. Consequently, a new and more ruthless war between north and south began in 1983. This soon coincided with drought and famine conditions prevalent thoughout the Horn of Africa. Unlike the starvation in Ethiopia, however, the Sudan's famine was largely ignored by the world's media. There was, however, an influx of world aid organizations and NGOs to Khartoum, and their workers were spread throughout the south trying to alleviate the starvation and destruction of war and famine. But the new government was reluctant to help the rebel enemy, except on its own rather narrow terms.

By 1986, the military wing of the new southern movement, the Sudanese People's Liberation Army (SPLA) under John Garang, had managed to unite various African tribal peoples in successful battles against the Sudan Army of the new leader Sadiq el Mahdi. The situation grew more critical that year as the war was being carried on by terrifying means on both sides, "a war without ethics," as Dr. Achol Deng of the Sudan Relief and Rehabilitation Association described it. The SPLA was burning the villages of those who did not support them, stealing their cattle, kidnapping children as army bearers, and raping the women. The government army and its militia were equally brutal, committing atrocities against captured SPLA soldiers and civilians, enslaving people, stealing grain, and halting aid trucks. A UN Operation Rainbow was organized to fly food aid to the south, but it failed when the government refused it permission to fly and the SPLA warned it would shoot down any aid plane—something it had already done that spring.

Thousands of southerners were jamming the towns and refugee camps or were fleeing to Ethiopia. By the beginning of 1988, with the drought growing more severe, women and children were dying by the hundreds every day in government garrison towns besieged by the SPLA. Food and medical supplies dwindled while aid groups in Khartoum begged the government to release the foodstuffs that were piling up there and at Port Sudan. But the Mahdi government invoked its rights as a sovereign nation to prevent the distribution of humanitarian aid; in areas of its state that it could not control, no other agency was to be allowed to operate.

In February 1988, the International Committee of the Red Cross had worked out an agreement to send food aid to the south. But it took until December to get it moving. By the end of that year it was estimated that as many as 250,000 people had died in southern Sudan as the result of war, starvation, and the use of food as a weapon by both sides. Those deaths were in addition to the 150,000 who had died by starvation and conflict over the three previous years.

The situation was so horrifying in the camps and besieged towns that, despite the Sudanese government's harassing actions, a number of NGOs started transporting food and medicines by truck or plane from Kenya, and even Uganda, into the south. But this was still only a drop in the bucket of need. When floods in the Khartoum area in August 1988 drew wide media attention, international concern and pressure for assistance to the south began to mount. The United Nations and the western nations were finally ready to act, and out of this grew Operation Lifeline Sudan (OLS).

Operation Lifeline Sudan

An Ethiopian-born peace activist and aid adviser, Abdul Mohammed, originated the idea of Operation Lifeline and played a lead role in assembling a research team to plan how it could be accomplished. The team worked out how much food should be delivered to what towns and camps in the south before the rainy season began and the best means of transport available. Meanwhile, UNICEF's James Grant, who was to be put in charge of the whole operation, had already won the reluctant agreement of Prime Minister Mahdi and, more important, his consent to contact the SPLA.

A major conference of UN organizations, donor countries, NGOs, and the Sudanese government was held in Khartoum in March 1989. An agreement was reached to deliver 156,000 tonnes of food and medical supplies, to save 100,000 starving people, during the month of April. To do this, both the government and the SPLA had to agree not to attack relief convoys, flights, or their personnel.

Larry Minear, who has written *A Critical Review of Operation Lifeline Sudan*, has said that the Sudanese government's agreement was important for the precedent it set in conceding sovereignty over some of its territory to the UN for humanitarian purposes. He told the conference: "It was an interesting set of negotiations because the United Nations was never able to get both parties into the same room." He referred to a picture of Grant negotiating with the SPLA's John Garang in remote Kongor, saying that it was "significant" because most UN officials "do not deal with insurgent forces. But in this case, on humanitarian grounds, Jim Grant took the initiative, sought out the SPLA, and got their agreement to the principle."

Initially the UN had sought a six-month cease-fire to deliver the aid, but they reduced it to a month. The SPLA rebels would not, however, agree to the "month of tranquillity" because they feared their troops would lose military momentum. So they would only agree to eight "corridors of tranquillity" by which the food and medicines could be sent to the south for one month, while fighting outside these narrow zones could carry on.

Building on what networks the ICRC and the NGOs had already established, the first UN food trucks set forth from Khartoum and Nairobi in April 1989. The first trainload of supplies steaming by rail to the south-west town of Aweil was attacked and UN personnel were severely mauled, but it got through. Barges with aid, sailing down the White Nile to Malakal, unarmed and flying the UN colours, were not interfered with, while huge Hercules cargo planes and Twin Otter light planes flew safely to the many landing strips in the south. One month was not nearly enough time to deliver the tonnage proposed to the dispersed towns and camps where the need was greatest, and in addition the rainy season began in May, wiping out many roads. But the operation was allowed to continue, although only five of the eight corridors granted by the SPLA stayed open. By the end of September, 97 per cent of the tonnage had been shipped to the region by the UN and ICRC and distributed by the NGOs, because both sides continued to observe the zonal cease-fires.

This does not mean it was smooth sailing. UN Secretary-General Javier Pérez de Cuellar later saluted "the remarkable courage and determination of the drivers, their support crews, and the UN/NGO escort teams. They have been confronted with mines, rocket attack, and automatic weapons fire, all aimed at clearly marked UN convoys. The images of drivers killed and wounded, UN escort leaders targeted for assassination, and abandoned, burned-out relief vehicles offer a sobering appreciation of the human cost Operation Lifeline Sudan has incurred in some of its humanitarian efforts."

This successful operation continued despite the toppling of the Mahdi government in June 1989 by Lieutenant General Omar Hasan el Bashir, who promptly pledged to continue Operation Lifeline. Although the cease-fires technically only applied to the corridors, Larry Minear told the conference, this had other effects. "The return of tranquillity to the corridors helped to reclaim for civilian use the roads, which had been the main arteries for overland military movements. Commerce which had thrived before the war along the roads began to flourish again, benefitting the surrounding countryside as well. With a perceptible decrease in tension and upswing in market activity, the enlarged corridors became, in effect, 'zones of peace.'"

Although the operation wound down in the fall of 1989, negotiations with the Bashir government and the SPLA finally resulted, at the end of March 1990, in the launch of Operation Lifeline 2. Despite the continuation of the war, the improvements in health brought about by Lifeline 1 encouraged aid people to provide more development help in the form of seeds, agricultural tools, and fishing equipment to improve living conditions in the war-torn areas.

Although the SPLA rebels seemed to feel the second operation was less neutral, less even-handed in its aid distribution than the first, an agreement for Operation Lifeline 3 was made in 1991 and was carried out, though less effectively.

While both sides can agree on the need for humanitarian aid to help the children and civilians, they still cannot agree to sit down at the same table to negotiate. Minear recalled that a meeting did take place in Nairobi in September 1990 "in which the leader of relief from the Khartoum side, the Commissioner of Relief and Rehabilitation, and the leader of the SPLA relief desk came together, but they just didn't talk to each other at all." So separate talks have to be carried on in an atmosphere of rumour, misapprehension, and suspicion. Minear added, however, that they both agree on helping their children and on some humanitarian principles: "It's a thin reed, but it's there."

Reviewing the lessons of Operation Lifeline Sudan, Larry Minear said that "the OLS did embody the principle that civilians caught in the crossfire do have a right to humanitarian assistance wherever they are located." But he noted that sensitizing military personnel about these rights had its difficulties. Pressure from UN and donor governments could convince Sudanese leaders and army officers. But "at one point when John Garang [SPLA leader] was in Washington meeting with NGOs, they made a strong pitch to him on behalf of citizens of Juba, which was surrounded by the SPLA and being fired on. Garang said, 'as a military man I will try to take Juba, but I will try to ensure there is no undue loss of civilian life.'" He was pressed about rights under the Geneva Convention and, according to Minear, "Garang said he could assure us they did not have in their field library in southern Sudan a copy of these international ground rules. But he said they will abide by the rules and would welcome the ICRC to come and teach them."

Aside from affirming the rights of civilians to aid in war zones, the Sudanese Lifeline also managed to bend long-held rules about national sovereignty. It worked to limit the invocation of sovereignty or the sanctity of internal affairs to block humanitarian activities. Minear said there needed to be changes in the existing humanitarian and political apparatus of the UN system if human needs in conflict zones are to be effectively addressed. For instance, he pointed out that UNICEF, from its earliest days, "has had an implicit, now an explicit mandate to deal with insurgent movements" without conveying any diplomatic recognition to the rebels. That was not the case for the World Food Programme or the UN Development Programme, both of which would find such a mandate of tremendous help in these conflict situations.

The lessons of Lifeline Sudan also apply to other situations. In his report on OLS, Minear noted that the key lessons from the Sudan were not so peculiar to that country "that they cannot be adapted to other circumstances, and strengthen the international community's ability to provide succour in other civil war settings. The lessons include the need for clarity regarding humanitarian principles, objectives and strategies; for leadership, both within the UN system and outside; for partnership among the aid actors, both external and indigenous; for institutional flexibility; and for linkages between humanitarian assistance and related concerns, such as human rights, development, and peace."

A Failure at Peacemaking

The Sudanese ambassador to the United States, Ahmed Abdulla, told the conference that while the OLS saved thousands of lives, "it did not resolve the conflict, but it did produce an improved atmosphere among the warring parties." It was not settled, he said, "because it was much deeper than the question of humanitarian aid." To Larry Minear that is not enough, for, as he says in his critical review, "the failure to exploit more fully the opening to advance the peace agenda, as was done in Afghanistan and Central America, represents a lost opportunity."[2]

In Afghanistan, UN-co-ordinated relief operations in what was called Operation Salam paralleled UN-facilitated peace negotiations that eventually ended the Soviet military intervention in that country. And in El Salvador, the UNICEF-inspired operation of "days of peace" for immunization of children helped ease the way for a more recent peace agreement to end the war. But Operation Lifeline was purely a humanitarian exercise carrying no peace initiative, for, as UNICEF's James Grant said, "I did not have peace in my mandate."

Minear told the conference that at the 1989 meeting in Khartoum which initiated the OLS the peace issue was raised. "Canada played a particularly key role in this," he said, "because the Canadians said right from the start that they were anxious to contribute humanitarian assistance to Sudan. But in their view, the real underlying problem was a political and military one, and that until progress was made in resolving the terms of conflict, the underlying struggle, no assistance beyond humanitarian aid might be provided." That could mean no developmental or military aid without action on peace.

This careful Canadian statement, much appreciated by other Western delegates, called attention to the fundamental issue and suggested an opportunity for Lifeline to provide some confidence-building among the parties that might help in the pursuit of peace. Even the Sudanese prime minister agreed with the merit of seeking to negotiate a long-term peace accord with the SPLA. Some efforts at negotiating through third parties was attempted, but without any success. The Operation failed to provide, as Minear put it, "a continuing and sustained process leading to political negotiations to settle the conflict."

In 1992, although Operation Lifeline 4 was scheduled to continue, that peace process seemed even farther away. There had been a split in the SPLA leadership, weakening its campaign, and the government had become more Islamic under pressure from the Muslim Brotherhood. Khartoum was aided by the fall of Ethiopia's Mengistu regime which cut off supplies to the Sudanese rebels. A major military offensive by the Sudan Army soon captured the principal SPLA towns of Pochala and Bor, the base where the rebellion began. This ruthless drive, aided by weaponry supplied by Iran, wrecked the relief aid operation.

At the same time, the saga of some 12,000 Dinka and Nuer boys, most of them war orphans, came to public attention. These children had fled to Ethiopian refugee camps to escape the war in southern Sudan. With Ethiopia's war over, they returned to Pochala, and now after four years of trekking and starving, they were being driven south to find a haven in a new camp on the Kenyan border. Their sad plight revealed again how the wars in the Horn of Africa affect everyone, but the children most of all.

IRAQ, IRAN, AND KUWAIT

The state of Iraq, under President Saddam Hussein, has been initially responsible for, and partially the site of, two major wars in the past 12 years. During the eight-year Iraq-Iran War that began in 1980, it is estimated that as many as 580,000 Iranians and about 400,000 Iraqis died, the bloodiest conflict since the Second Great War. In the recent Gulf War following Iraq's invasion of Kuwait, some 250,000 Iraqis were killed along with 342 coalition soldiers, not to mention the thousands of civilian deaths as a result of the U.S.-led aerial bombardment. Humanitarianism in the defence of children was not a priority in either of these wars, but one effort was briefly successful during the Gulf War.

The Historical Background

The land of Iraq, site of Babylon and Nineveh of the great Assyrian empires and often called the "cradle of civilization," was a poverty-stricken leftover of the Ottoman empire when it achieved independence from a British mandate in 1932. It devolved from a royal regime to several military ones, until the revolution of 1968 brought the Arab Ba'ath socialist party to power. From that bloody coup, Saddam Hussein eventually thrust his way to the top, where he has remained ever since.

Saddam Hussein and his close followers were Sunni Muslims, a minority in Iraq. But they were ruthless with opponents, either in the Ba'ath party or in opposition, gradually eliminating anyone who dissented. There were public executions and televised hangings. Hussein established a police state, with both state and military secret police responsible only to the Mukhabarat, the police network of the party. Under a 1977 law, any person opposing the Ba'athist revolution could be deprived of citizenship. By murder and by law, the Communist party and the underground that fought for the rights of the Shiite Muslim majority were destroyed, and the

Kurdish minority was kept in check. The result was, as Iraqi writer Samir al-Khalil has said, a "republic of fear" where the Ba'ath party turned "fear into the glue of the Iraqi body politic."[3]

Saddam Hussein, whose country possessed one of the world's great oil reserves, now nationalized the oil firms and began leading his subdued population with the carrot of social welfare. With the new found oil wealth, he provided free health care and education, so that Iraq became one of the most literate countries in the Third World. He built up the country's infrastructure with paved roads, bridges, rural electrification, and water-purification plants. He spent money on new technology, science, and much modern military weaponry. Because he was to host the conference of the Non-Aligned Movement in 1982 and hoped to take over its Third World leadership from Fidel Castro, he embarked on a massive build-up of Baghdad, hoping to make it the new Babylon. Five new modern hotels, huge urban renewal projects, a hastily constructed subway development, four-lane roads, and new parks were built, along with a monumental marble memorial to the Iraqi revolutionary heroes, featuring an adulatory exhibition of the life of Saddam Hussein.

In his megalomania, Hussein decided to take on that other single-minded leader of the region, Iran's Ayatollah Khomeini. Super-confident that his huge army of the "republic of fear" could knock out the chaotic clerical regime of the "republic of faith" in two weeks, Hussein invaded Iran on September 20, 1980. Instead, it lasted eight long years because neither dictatorial leader would give up. In the course of it, Iran's clerical fundamentalists introduced the ugly concept of children as mine-sweepers and "holy warriors." For his part, Hussein, posing as the kindly, modern warrior, the new Nebuchadnezzar, was seen every night on TV kissing little girls or clapping manly little boys on the cheek as their mothers handed over the family jewelry for his war effort. There were no humanitarian cease-fires during this bloodbath.

The Iraqi leader came out of the war in 1988 heavily indebted, his oil ports on the Persian Gulf destroyed, yet with his best troops and air force largely intact through the sacrifice of his militia and strategic dispersal of his aircraft, a tactic he used again in the Gulf War. Since Western nations had armed him heavily during the Iran war as a hedge against a Khomeini victory, Hussein must have felt he could absorb Kuwait, whose excellent Gulf harbour he needed, without too much trouble.

Kuwait, a minor Gulf sheikdom until it struck oil in 1938, had been an autonomous district of the Ottoman empire for two centuries. Independent Iraq had long coveted it, but Hussein's invasion and annexation of this wealthy state in August 1990 caught the world by surprise. The result was the Gulf War, which began officially in January 1991 after the United Nations had condemned the invasion and imposed sanctions for less than six months. The Americans, impatient to act with force when oil was at stake, had built up a coalition of Western and Arab nations with sufficient troops to attack the Iraqi invader. Abandoning the sanctions route and the idea of a UN army, the U.S.-led air offensive set out to destroy Iraq's military bases and civilian infrastructure, which it largely did. Then a short, bloody ground battle followed and this so-called "high tech" war was over in 43 days by March 1991. Kuwait was liberated.

The "Bubble of Tranquillity"

In the course of the air war, efforts were made to provide medical and food relief to the Iraqi people. The two humanitarian relief convoys that tried to drive from Amman in Jordan to Baghdad were hit by coalition bombardment and had to turn back. But a Teheran-based effort conceived by Richard Reid, UNICEF's regional director in Amman, and other UNICEF and World Health Organization (WHO) officials succeeded.

Dr. Eric Hoskins, medical co-ordinator for the Gulf Peace team, described the operation at the conference. "They put together a team of five or six experts [from UNICEF and WHO] to deliver some relief supplies to Iraq and to assess the situation of the civilian population there. They had a convoy of about a dozen trucks to drive the road between Teheran and Baghdad. They obtained approval beforehand from the Iraqi administration and the U.S. administration. The convoy was very clearly marked and the exact time of its crossing the Iraqi border was widely publicized. It was agreed that the convoy as it moved would not be attacked. It was not a corridor or zone [of peace] but this entity that was protected. So that's where the term 'bubble of tranquillity' came up."

The "bubble convoy" arrived in Baghdad unscathed on February 16 as the war continued, even on the road it had just passed through. According to the UN sanctions regulations, only certain medical supplies could be transported, and no food. The supplies were duly delivered to the Iraqi authorities.

"The second component of the initiative," Hoskins said, "was to carry out a brief assessment for several days in Baghdad itself." They were also able to travel to Falluja, about a one-hour drive out of Baghdad. They worked closely with the ministry of health and the ministry of social affairs, who took them around to various sites. In Baghdad they found that "there was virtually no electricity; it was reduced to about 4 per cent of pre-war levels. There was very little pumped water; people had to get it from the river or break into pipes to get it. Sewage was backing up because there was no electricity to pump it out. Hospitals and patients were suffering because of lack of medicines; because of a lack of fuel and spare parts they could not maintain generators. There were difficulties with transportation. Dangers with unexploded bombs and shortages of gasoline meant patients could not get to hospitals. Food prices were very, very high, as much as 100 times what they had been pre-war. And communications had broken down completely."

UNICEF's Richard Reid asked the press, following his mission to Baghdad: "Does an entire country have to be left 'brain-dead?' " He said Baghdad was a city "essentially unmarked, a body with its skin basically intact, with every main bone broken and with its joints and tendons cut.... The health system is collapsing. There are no phones and no electricity and no petrol and only a people reduced to daily improvisations and scrounging." He wondered whether an entire country had to be crippled to enforce a principle, presumably the rarely exercised UN principle of collective security to suppress aggression and the annexation of independent states.

Reid and others wrote a report on the Iraqi situation for the UN secretary-general, who passed it, with its recommendations, to the sanctions committee of the Security Council. "It was the first time that the international community could look at the consequences of the war," said Dr. Hoskins. In mid-March 1991, "those recommendations were accepted by the Security Council, which led in turn to the declaration of a humanitarian emergency in Iraq. That allowed emergency food to go in for the first time since August 1990." Because the war was then over, it went in by road from Amman and from Turkey.

The UN declaration also allowed the importation of medicines, and items like chlorine and water-purification tablets. Unfortunately, as Dr. Hoskins pointed out, the UN's offer to Iraq to allow it to sell its oil and use the revenue for food and medicine in this emergency has not been taken up. Iraq has refused to accept UN supervision of its oil sales, even if its people die as a consequence. The U.S. and the UN coalition have said that until there is an agreement they will offer Iraq nothing else. By late 1992 the two sides were still at an impasse and Saddam Hussein was effectively allowing relief organizations to assume the public-health burden in Iraq, inadequate as that was. Hussein has survived, as Michael Ignatieff put it in *The Observer*, "by using his own people as hostages and by doing his best to exploit our conscience."

Aftermath of the War

Dr. Hoskins was coordinator of the Harvard Study Team of 90 researchers that went to Iraq in August 1991 to study more than 9,000 Iraqi households. It found a grim situation, with the death rate of children under five tripled since pre-war days. Slightly under one million children under five were estimated to be malnourished. There were epidemics of cholera, typhoid, and meningitis. The shortages of medicines went on, with hospitals able to get only about 10 per cent of the medicines they had pre-war. Surgery was carried on with a minimum of anaesthetic or none. With inflation nearing 2,000 per cent and incomes one-twentieth of what they were before the war, the health and well-being of all the Iraqi people were greatly endangered. It was later estimated by the Harvard team that between January and August 1991 some 49,600 children under five years of age died as an indirect effect of the bombing, civilian uprisings, and the UN economic embargo.

Dr. Hoskins was highly critical of the UN's use of force to liberate Kuwait. "With great certainty, had we not resorted to war, 50,000 Iraqi children would not have died." He also questioned the UN trade-off of food for oil, saying that the world body, created as an instrument of peace, "for the first time approved the use of food as a weapon against innocent civilians in the war zones."

Another equally serious aftermath of the Gulf War inside Iraq was the uprising of oppressed Shiites and Kurds, who had been publicly encouraged by President Bush's call to Iraqis to overthrow Saddam Hussein. This ill-considered appeal to desperate people forced nearly two million Kurds from their homes as Iraqi forces tried to put down the revolt, while uncounted thousands of Shiites in the south were massacred by troops or fled into the vast marshes of the Tigris and the Euphrates. The Kurdish people, a minority in Iraq as well as in neighbouring Iran and Turkey, have been fighting oppression and for a Kurdistan for the past 45 years. But this revolt, with the terrible conditions imposed upon Kurdish women and children in desolate mountain camps in Turkey and Iran, forced the UN and the U.S. to act with at least some humanitarian assistance. The Americans flew in troops to build and protect camps in northern Iraq after the UN Security Council passed Resolution 688, which ignored Iraqi sovereignty and insisted that Iraq immediately allow access to its territory to provide UN humanitarian assistance to the desperate Kurdish refugees. Although Saddam Hussein was stubbornly refusing to allow the UN to control the sale of his oil for humanitarian relief for his own desperate people because it would "infringe on Iraq's sovereignty," there was little he could do about this demand by the UN, backed by American forces. He had already acquiesced to another UN resolution permitting UN officials to investigate and destroy Iraq's nuclear weapons facilities and chemical weapons stockpiles. These unusual United Nations' actions, bending the traditional views of territorial integrity, have opened up a widespread debate.

Meanwhile the tragedy of the Kurds has continued. Hundreds of their villages have been destroyed, thousands are still in UN camps; Iraqi troops have harassed the Kurdish forces and built a 560-kilometre military line across northern Iraq to enforce an economic blockade of hundreds of thousands of Kurds. Negotiations between Saddam Hussein and Kurdish leaders were still stalled in 1993. The Iraqi leader was playing for time, hoping UN aid teams and U.S. forces around the region would leave and he could then crush the Kurds, as he has done so often before. Meanwhile his troops in the south were trying to destroy the Shiite rebels caught in the famed marshlands of the Tigris and the Euphrates.

While the UN continued to enforce its important demilitarization resolutions, it was also able, in the fall of 1992, to persuade Iraq to allow UN food aid convoys to enter during the winter months to supply the food-short Kurds, an operation that was continually harassed by the Iraqis. For the equally desperate Shiites in the marshes, there was only the American-inspired "no-fly zone," where Iraqi warplanes were prohibited from operating. This provided no help to those Shiites trapped under artillery bombardment there. The jousting between Hussein and Bush continued into 1993 with little consideration for suffering Kurds, Shiites, or Iraqis.

Although Dr. Hoskins and others at the conference felt the UN sanctions should be removed, Hoskins did say the "bubble of tranquillity" was "an important example of a humanitarian cease-fire, even though it might be the barest minimum of one." It had no obvious, immediate peacebuilding impact, he said, but it served as a catalyst to get the UN humanitarian emergency declaration proclaimed, thus making people around the world recognize that there was a humanitarian catastrophe occurring in Iraq: "It puts the human side of the conflict on the UN agenda." As such, it was one initiative worth pursuing.

Part Three

WAR-TORN WORLD:
The Troubled Search for Peace

I come from a culture where solving conflict is a day to day thing. I lived in a rural area before I came here, and my tribe always ended up at war with a neighbouring tribe. The way we solved conflicts was: my chief would call in the enemy tribe for a peace visit party. We would have a big party, bring the other tribe in, get together, and then for one evening we would stop the tribal fighting. Let them sit down with us, have dinner, talk to each other. After the feast and exchange of gifts, we would tell them, okay, go away and if you still want to fight, come tomorrow morning and we'll meet you on the battlefield.

And most often it worked out that after we sat down together and talked about things, nobody wanted to fight. It seemed as if we had formed some kind of invisible link with each other. And the message I'm trying to get across is, we cannot solve the world's conflicts overnight. The only way we can solve these problems is by getting the two conflicting parties together.

Sandis Dick, from Papua-New Guinea, student at the Lester B. Pearson College of the Pacific, Victoria, B.C.

Would that humanitarian cease-fires and conflict resolution could be attained in such a civilized way, over the dinner table! But unfortunately in the world today, it is not so easy, and there are often more than two parties involved. The Centre for Days of Peace, which convened the conference, identified eight conflict zones in which humanitarian cease-fires might have a chance of succeeding. The following reports are based in part on conference discussions about the possibilities of what has been and can be done.

Horn of Africa:
ETHIOPIA/ERITREA

The 30-year war that ravaged Ethiopia and Eritrea from 1961 to 1991 was both a civil war and a war of liberation. Ethiopia is the only country in Africa that escaped direct colonial transformation, although it was occupied by the Italians from 1935-41. For nearly 2000 years its feudal dynasties, born by legend out of the union of King Solomon and the Queen of Sheba, continued to hold power as the Abyssinian empire. The myth of Prester John ruling this Christian kingdom in isolation fascinated the West from the sixth century onwards. "The continuity of Ethiopian history was unbroken by external intervention for over a millennium, leaving aside the Italian interlude," as one writer put it.

The Historical Background
In the scramble for Africa by the imperial powers in the late nineteenth-century, Ethiopia's new borders were imposed by the Italians, the French, and the British. And it was the eventual disposition of the colony that Italy had made out of Eritrea which would lead to war and revolution in Ethiopia.

In the 1880s, Italy began to colonize Ethiopia's coastal province of Eritrea, which forms the north-east border and, along with the French enclave of Djibouti, cuts Ethiopia off from the Red Sea. Italy held onto this territory until the Second World War, when Britain took it over in 1941. Eritrea prospered politically, economically, and socially under these two colonial powers, unlike Ethiopia, which was under the autocratic regime headed by Emperor Haile Selassie. After the British rule, the federation of Eritrea and Ethiopia was considered by the UN and pushed by the United States, which wanted a communications base in the capital city of Asmara. In 1952 the UN turned the country over to Ethiopia as a federal unit, without any consultation with the Eritreans. Ignoring the UN settlement, Emperor Selassie imposed autocratic rule, pillaged its economy and factories, and in 1962 incorporated the country formally. By this time, the Eritreans were already up in arms and the war of liberation had begun.

Emperor Selassie, the Lion of Judah, who had won the world's admiration but no support for standing up to Benito Mussolini's brutal occupation of 1936, learned little after the Second World War about dealing with the problems of the downtrodden peasant farmers in his regained realm. His land reforms were such a failure that in 1973 his country faced another of its devastating cyclical famines. Even though the Eritrean Liberation Front was split by its Marxist wing, the war with Eritrea continued. The example of resistance to the Emperor was spreading, especially among the many well-educated Eritreans in the Ethiopian government and army. In 1974, students demonstrated in Addis Ababa, young officers led a revolt of the army, and with a minimum of bloodshed installed a revolutionary regime and ousted the King of Kings.

The Derg, the military committee now running the new Ethiopia, soon exhibited a Marxist orientation and by 1976 was pursuing all-out war with Eritrea. In this chaotic state of affairs, others saw opportunity. Some radicals in Tigre province, unhappy with new land reforms favouring southern Ethiopia and dissatisfied with the Derg's lack of commitment to Marxist programs, began their rebellion against the centre. Since Tigreans and Afars in that province were relatives to similar groups in Eritrea, they were soon co-operating with the left-wing Eritreans in the war against the Derg. Complicating the problems of the Ethiopian regime in 1977-78 were the Somalis, who took this occasion to invade the disputed south-east grazing lands of the Ogaden. The Derg survived this brief war with the help of military aid from the Soviet Union and troops from Castro's Cuba.

Taking advantage of the internal struggles that developed in the

Ethiopian regime, one man rose to the top in 1978: Mengistu Haile Mariam. Under his dictatorial leadership a surfeit of weapons was provided to the armed forces. His wasteful celebration of the tenth anniversary of the revolution, in 1984, coincided with the worst famine in recent history, one that brought world attention to his neglect of the children dying horribly in refugee camps while his troops attacked aid caravans and halted supplies. During the 1984 famine in Ethiopia, according to Dr. Achol Marial Deng of the Sudan Relief and Rehabilitation Association, "the Orthodox church and the Muslim churches kept silent when everyone was dying," and they lost their legitimacy as providers of aid.

Channels for Humanitarian Aid

Dr. Solomon Gidada of Addis Ababa recounted the measures taken to counter this terrible emergency: "It started in 1984 when the famine was hitting Tigre and Wollo provinces and children were dying everywhere. So we asked, Why can't the churches organize a lifeline? The Catholic church had a network of organizations in Tigre and my church (Protestant) had an organization in government-held areas in Wollo. So we formed action groups and linked up, along with two aid organizations. We were operating on the principle of the right of food for all [i.e. food should not be used as a political weapon]. We established 70 distribution points in Tigre and a relief corridor to Massawa."

Dr. Gidada described the whole region as a grey area, in the sense that no cease-fire was obtained. Wollo was out of bounds, but "you just go in, and once you start you keep going. If they bomb us, we will tell the world." They contacted the major embassies in Addis Ababa and got their help: $50 million was raised in Geneva; the British helped repair bridges; and the road from Massawa, the Eritrean port on the Red Sea, through to Tigre and Wollo was kept open for food relief to the starving children.

The Joint Relief Partnership

By 1987, this co-operative operation was called the Joint Relief Partnership (JRP), and it included the country's largest church, the Ethiopian Orthodox. The vast properties and monasteries of this ancient Coptic state church, representing 20 million adherents and formerly headed by the Emperor, had been taken over by the revolutionary government. It had little experience in social welfare work, but once it realized the need, it worked eagerly together with the smaller churches.

Canada's ambassador to Ethiopia from 1986 to 1988, David Macdonald, now a member of Parliament, attended the Ottawa conference and described this linking of the churches in the Joint Relief Partnership as "an historic breakthrough." He said the churches fortunately decided to keep the co-operation going after the first famine conditions had been relieved, because there was an even more dramatic need in 1989-90. At that time, the war was turning against the Mengistu government. As Macdonald said, "Since a substantial portion of both Tigre and Wollo were controlled by the rebel factions, the government could not authorize, or even assist anybody getting into that area. So the churches said,'Look, we know all sides. We are prepared to announce that we are going to move in there.' With the informal acceptance of all sides, they were allowed to put together an incredible lifeline to the north that lasted for a full year," a year when 85 per cent of the crop failed.

Nothing was put on paper. The combatants did not sit down together. According to Macdonald, "They simply said to the key military people on each side: 'This is what we plan to do.' They didn't ask for their approval. They said: 'We simply expect you to respect us in trying to get food through to the people.' At any point, either side could have shut it down or fired on any truck." So the Joint Relief Partnership used trucks marked with a special church relief flag, and they operated from Assab, a port on the Red Sea in

Eritrea, across to Dessie in Wollo and up north to Tigre. According to Macdonald, they moved "ten thousand tonnes a month, and millions of people were kept alive by that operation."

A Canadian parliamentary delegation that visited Dessie in January 1991 and saw the JRP in action reported that "at the beginning, it was a risky and doubtful operation. It started with 11 trucks and nine months later, with 230 trucks, celebrated the delivery of 100,000 tonnes of food."[1] Dr. Gidada summed it up by saying that "the Joint Relief Partnership was, for Ethiopia, more important than Operation Lifeline Sudan, because it was not imposed from outside." It was totally indigenous, put together by local churches and local people who knew the ground and the combatants. Early on, even the Mengistu regime recognized their importance by including the heads of all the churches in their newly formed parliament.

In the war in Ethiopia and Eritrea, there was little communication across the front lines, no talking to the enemy, no cease-fires — no hope for a peaceful settlement. The conflict was resolved by force of arms. By the end of 1990, the tenacious and efficient fighters of the Eritrean People's Liberation Front and the Ethiopian People's Democratic Front had the demoralized Ethiopian government troops on the run. By May of 1991 they had forced Mengistu to flee the country, and they entered Addis Ababa in a relatively bloodless take-over. David Macdonald believes that the co-operative effort of the Joint Relief Partnership probably helped to bring about a more orderly transfer of power in an atmosphere of general relief, rather than the expected bitter, last-ditch battle in the streets of the capital.

The transitional government of Ethiopia, headed by Meles Zenawi, was given two years to dismantle the Mengistu war machine, develop a democratic system of government, and organize a free market economy in the midst of rebuilding the wartorn country. In the spring of 1993 a referendum on independence was held and the people voted for a free Eritrea. The task of the new Ethiopian regime is hampered by the rise of ethnic disorder and banditry in the countryside, and by the continuing effects of drought and malnutrition. Elections are promised for 1994, but already tribal divisions are splitting this former Communist fiefdom.

But, as David Macdonald said, "the problems of Ethiopia will not be satisfactorily solved until the problems of Sudan and Somalia and Djibouti are resolved. It is very serious. As Somalia grows more totally chaotic, it has a profound and destabilizing effect on Ethiopia, and the longer that goes on the more dangerous it gets for Ethiopia."

Horn of Africa: SOMALIA

The civil conflict in Somalia, so long ignored by the outside world, finally won the active attention of the United Nations in 1992. Unfortunately, it took the continued slaughter of men, women, and children in the capital city of Mogadishu and the death of thousands in famine conditions in the countryside, publicized at last by the world's media and by frustrated aid groups, to force the international community to grapple with this complex situation. As Dr. Hussein Adam, associate professor of political science at Holy Cross College, in Worcester, Massachusetts, told the Ottawa conference: "Somalis feel Somalia is treated like a leper in the international community."

How did such a crisis develop in this pastoral country that lies like a crescent around the south-east corner of Ethiopia, washed by the blue waters of the Indian Ocean and the Gulf of Aden?

The Historical Background

Unique among the peoples of the Horn of Africa, the Somalis have belonged to a single nation state since 1960. Their people use the same language, are from the same race, and largely share the same Muslim religion. When the nineteenth-century colonial powers greedily sliced up the continent between them, the northern part of Somalia was taken over by the British in 1885 and called British Somaliland, while the next year Italy obtained the larger slice to the south and called it Italian Somaliland. During the Second World War, the British took over the whole of Somalia and occupied it until 1949, when the United Nations placed the south under Italian trusteeship. Independence was achieved for both halves in 1960 when a plebiscite was held and it was agreed to unite the country as Somalia.

Elected republican government lasted until 1969, when the country was taken over in a military coup. A Supreme

Revolutionary Council was headed by General Mohamed Siad Barre, who dissolved the national assembly and suspended the constitution. His 21-year rule began with some progressive measures, such as the introduction of a written language for the first time. But he also began to agitate amongst the various tribal clans that make up Somalia for the formation of a Greater Somalia, urging the return of Ogaden province from Ethiopia and Djibouti from the French. This was contrary to the principle upheld by the Organization of African Unity that all African states should maintain the old colonial boundaries to avoid unending wars.

President Barre began to seek military aid from the Soviet Union and in 1976 established the Somali Socialist Revolutionary Party as the basis of a one-party state, with himself as dictator. His expansionist aims became clear in 1977 when his troops invaded Ogaden. Having earlier broken relations with the Soviet Union, Barre now faced an Ethiopia buttressed with Soviet aid and Cuban troops, and in early 1978 Somali forces were driven out of the Ogaden in defeat. But in the process, Barre had won the military support of Western nations, especially the United States, which, between 1986 and 1988 would provide Barre with $100 million in military and economic aid. The quid pro quo, at that time, was American use of the strategic naval port of Berbera on the Gulf of Aden. Most of the economic aid Somalia now received was directed by Barre to the south, where 60 per cent of the population lives.

As an example of how everything in the Horn of Africa seems to be linked, in 1982, after Ethiopia and Somalia signed a treaty of peace, Somali refugees in Ethiopia, now well armed by the Mengistu regime, returned to the north. These members of the Isaaq clan began a rebellion against Barre's government and formed the Somali National Movement (SNM). Barre's forces retaliated, and in 1988 they launched a devastating aerial bombardment using mercenary pilots hired from Zimbabwe. Hargeisa, the largest city in the north, was 90 per cent destroyed, "an eerie-looking town without roofs," as one journalist put it. The SNM forces maintained control over the countryside, and in 1990 the largest tribe in the south, the Hawiye, also rose up against Barre. After a bloody battle with Barre's own Red Beret guards, they drove the aging dictator out of Mogadishu in January 1991.

Though the beaten Barre was now holed up with his troops in his own small clan area near the Kenyan border, peace did not return to Somalia. An interim president, Hawiye clan member Ali Mahdi Mohammed, was hastily selected by some politicians of the United Somali Congress and installed at Djibouti. The process was called illegal and not recognized by all the squabbling elements in anarchic Mogadishu, many of them newly armed with Barre's huge stockpile of weapons.

Some 20,000 people, many of them women and children, died in the struggle to liberate Somalia from Barre. The fighting was so indiscriminate that even aid people were being shot, and UNICEF pulled its workers out of Mogadishu early in 1991. Only a few aid and medical workers remained to help.

The Republic of Somaliland

In May 1991, led by the Somali National Movement, northerners who had returned to their devastated homes declared their independence. They now called the north the Republic of Somaliland, whose borders followed those of the old British Somaliland. In August, Dr. Hussein Adam, a northerner, visited the new republic, which had not yet achieved official international recognition. "The situation I found was that in northern Somalia they had a terrible shortage of things, and the city of Hargeisa had been almost 90 per cent destroyed. But they disarmed those young people they had used to fight the government, returned forces to barracks, and you could walk the city at night feeling secure.

"In the north there was peace, stability, and a de facto government, unlike Mogadishu. I travelled a lot in the countryside, in public transport, and it was extremely peaceful. I went to visit practically all the towns and cities in the north." (Even the town of Borama, which non-Isaaq tribesmen had claimed was destroyed by SNM forces, was, he later said, not damaged badly at all.)

"It is amazing to say this, but in Somalia then, it was the urban people in the north who were suffering and dying rather than the rural people. The reason is because the wars were aimed at the cities. The people of Hargeisa, when it was being bombed by air, ran away to the countryside as refugees and lost everything. The rural people remained there. They depend on the rains, and the last year or two the rains were good. In the city, houses were destroyed, so they needed cement, wood, nails, and corrugated iron for the roofs. These things were all taken by the army and sold in Ethiopia and other places." Dr. Adam added that the army, which held out to the end in 10 per cent of the city, had left the houses mined, and this was delaying the return of the populace, who often lived in cardboard shacks awaiting mine-demolition teams who arrived in July. The refugee camps in the north were being run by UNICEF and other aid agencies and were well managed after several years of operation.

Mogadishu Slaughter

In Mogadishu, meanwhile, intermittent warfare continued, along with looting of aid stockpiles. Starvation became more serious, while water and power were largely cut off. On November 17, the forces of General Mohamed Farrah Aidid, chairman of the United Somali Congress and also a member of the Hawiye tribe, rebelled with force against interim president Ali Mahdi, and the capital city became a major killing ground as Aidid attempted to oust his rival from power.

The appalling slaughter that ensued as these two men of sub-clans of the same tribe fought for power was, as usual, suffered by the children and non-combatants of this once attractive city. Africa Watch estimated that, between November 1991 and February

1992, some 14,000 people were killed and 27,000 wounded by the mortar and tank shells, the automatic weapons fire, and the insidious mines. Everything lootable was stripped from houses, offices, and factories as roaming fighters sought items to sell to buy food, or raided stores or even aid agencies where food was kept. Little outside food aid was coming into the country, allegedly because agencies under the UN aegis felt it was too dangerous. Only a handful of medical aid workers remained in the second month of 1992: the ICRC, Médecins sans Frontières, Save the Children, and the SOS children's village on the outskirts of the city. Half a million of Somalia's 4.5 million people began facing starvation in February, according to U.S. aid officials, and crude refugee camps sprang up outside the city to house some 400,000 who fled the fighting. While the international community dithered as to how to get aid in, or how to get the combatants to cease fire, the casualties, 90 per cent of them non-combatants, continued to rise.

Scenes like these were far too common. From *The New York Times* in December:

A young victim is 5-year-old Mohamed Abvakar, who lay in the hot sun of the hospital grounds today, wincing from pain, the stump of his amputated right leg wrapped in a blood-soaked bandage. Nearby, 13-year-old Saeed Farah was dumped onto the sand outside the operating room by medical staff, blood oozing from a fresh and deep bullet wound in his head. The boy could not survive, said a doctor, who administered a painkiller to ease his death.

From the *Toronto Star* in February:

It takes all the strength Miishani Mohamed has left just to open her eyes. This 7-year-old lies asleep in a dirty nightgown, slowly starving to death. Since the latest round in Somalia's civil war began three months ago, Miishani has survived on nothing more than water, tea, and the odd scrap of bread.

Her once supple skin is drawn taught around her skull like shrunken leather, turning her innocent child's face into a horrific death mask.

Sister Maria Antonia Pira, an Italian nun trying to feed thousands of hungry Somali children and their mothers at the SOS village, pauses by her bed and softly calls her name. The child's lashes slowly flutter as she struggles to see, but only slices of white show. But she tries again, her emaciated body perfectly still as every ounce of will is concentrated on waking up. When her eyes finally open wide, they are frozen in terror. "What a poor creature," Sister Maria says, shaking her head, "It's too much when they come in this condition."

Abdul Mohammed of the Inter-Africa Group, who was promoting a heads-of-state summit for Horn of Africa nations, told the Ottawa conference that "the whole issue of humanitarian help is only taken up by outsiders, not, to our shame, by us." Yet several of the Somali delegates to the working group on Somalia insisted that Somali cultural values must be maintained and foreign intervention discouraged so the local people could solve their own problems.

Osman Mohammed, chief of the Somali National Movement's office in London, told the working group: "In Somalia, the clan warfare aim is not to save children first, but themselves." In areas where there had been five years of conflict and heavy loss of life, "the last point of importance was children. The common denominator was survival of the clan." Dr. Chris Giannou, who worked in Somalia in 1990 and again in 1992 agreed, saying that "the extended family unit is the important one in Somalia, so that peacebuilding for children is not so important." Osman Mohammed insisted that if a cease-fire is to be both effective and beneficial, "both sides should see an advantage. But you, coming from overseas, have lofty ideas. You have God, your concept of life based on your upbringing, based on your Christian values, based on the love of man — all these things mean nothing to me. I come from a different culture. I value my camel. I can go out with my camel to the other side of the country, find water and live with it. So outside interference should understand the cultural values and proceed with the acceptance of the local people." In the end, he conceded that the tribes' survival depends on protecting their young, but by that he meant the male children who would be the future warriors.

It is part of the legacy of Siad Barre's rule that he has sown distrust among the clans. Somalis — individualistic nomads of impressive stamina, aggressive, proud of their military prowess — are also extremely clannish. Barre adopted a divide-and-rule policy, encouraging each clan to compete against the other. Neither side in Mogadishu prevailed and even in the north, tribal clashes continued.

In late February 1992, the United Nations obtained an agreement between some representatives of the two sides in Mogadishu for a truce. UN Under-Secretary James Jonah saw the agreement as the result of the new mood in the UN Security Council that allowed for more UN involvement in internal disputes with international ramifications, and as the result of the election of former Egyptian foreign minister Boutros Boutros-Ghali as UN secretary-general, a diplomat who has dealt with many Somali problems. Yet despite the UN accord, sporadic fighting continued in Mogadishu. There was no government, no police force, no garbage collection, no electricity, no telephones, and no water in this lawless capital of Somalia.

Winds of Change

Dr. Hussein Adam alleged that the Italians, by supporting interim president Ali Mahdi, have contributed to the impasse. He said the UN would need to talk to more local representatives to reconcile the two sides. Because the fighting had been so bitter and bloody, there would need to be a reconciliation of all the tribes. There would also have to be another conference to decide on a legal interim president. And then, eventually, there would have to be a dialogue between the north and the south to see whether separate countries or a federation might be the solution for Somalia. It would all take time, and a foreign intervention, especially with troops, would not be productive, he felt, even if Mahdi might support such a move. In short, a humanitarian cease-fire in Mogadishu, while obviously urgently needed, did not seem to be in sight.

Yusef Ali Sheikh Madar, foreign minister of the new Republic of Somaliland, told the Ottawa conference: "I think there is a new wind of change in Africa at the moment. There is growing pressure that really is in the direction of overthrowing all dictators. The euphoria of the 1960s created nationalistic leaders who really tried to remain life presidents, and the only way to remove them was by the bullet. But we are witnessing democratic means of getting rid of our dictators, and the last one to leave was the president of Zambia, Kenneth Kaunda. In the Horn, it has been different. We have removed our dictators by the bullet because that was their language. But the future is one of hope for political change, with two new countries, Eritrea and Somaliland." Despite all the environmental destruction and displacement of people, he hoped Somaliland could create a stable and law-abiding society. "The new breed of leaders," he concluded, "should be responsive to the needs of the people." And, he added, open to "Africanizing" the new ideas as discussed at this conference.

Abdul Mohammed spoke of the emergence of new leaders, "the children of war," who planned a meeting for heads of state in 1992. "Participants at the meeting [in Addis Ababa] will include political leaders, opposition leaders, and rebel groups who will explore humanitarian issues within the context of the reality of the Horn of Africa. It is our hope that we can extract a commitment from these leaders, at the highest level, on the issues that have been eluding our region, and to institutionalize these solutions. For a change the solutions and focus will be directed from the people in the Horn... not outsiders."

That summit was held in Addis Ababa in April 1992 with leaders from Ethiopia, Eritrea, the Sudan, Djibouti, and Kenya in attendance. Somali leaders, however, were unable to come, though conference organizers hoped to get representatives of the north and south to sign later. They pledged to work together to end the Somali civil war and called on the warring factions in Mogadishu to observe the UN truce. They set up "a standing, high-level Horn-of-Africa committee to seek a solution to the conflict."

In an unusual development, while urging the combatants in Mogadishu to allow the delivery of urgently needed food and medical aid to the populace, the Addis Ababa summit pledged to consider establishing "corridors of tranquillity" so that humanitarian relief convoys could reach civilians in combat zones throughout the Horn of Africa. A sensible idea seemed to be catching on in a region of desperation.

By June 1992, a shaky truce had actually been achieved in Mogadishu, and some aid was being delivered by the Red Cross and the UN by sea and by air. But the airport was not secure, ship landings were hazardous, food was hijacked, and drought was helping to spread starvation throughout the country. Despite appeals from UN Secretary-General Boutros-Ghali, the Security Council was at odds about sending UN armed troops to protect relief workers so the aid could be delivered to the needy.

Some UN peacekeepers were sent in but they were ineffective in the face of total anarchy. Roving gangs of highly armed thugs terrorized the towns and countryside and pillaged the aid centres. It was only in November 1992, by which time some 300,000 Somali children, elderly, and other non-combatants had died of starvation, that U.S. President George Bush offered nearly 30,000 armed troops to bring order by force so aid could begin to reach the starving in regular fashion.

This unique UN enforcement operation — led not by the UN's "blue berets" but by UN-co-ordinated troops from the United

States, Canada, France, Italy and elsewhere — produced a kind of humanitarian cease-fire by armed intervention. It established corridors of relative peace by which aid convoys could reach those in need, and it attempted to disarm the roving bandits. Regular UN peacekeepers were then to take their place.

Meanwhile, under UN auspices, General Aideed and Ali Mahdi pledged to stop fighting, and the major clans began meetings in early 1993 to try to bring peace to this devastated country. A governing authority was the ultimate aim, but whether it would include the already peaceful and functioning northern Somaliland government would be another problem for the future.

MOZAMBIQUE

When it comes to cruel and obscene wars, it is very hard to surpass the grisly, irrational conflict that tore Mozambique apart for 17 years. Mozambique now may be one of the world's poorest countries, but it was once a rich agricultural colony of the Portuguese.

The Historical Background

The shadow of imperial Portugal hung over Mozambique from the time Vasco da Gama visited its coast in 1498 and encouraged the establishment of trading posts en route to India. The Portuguese made a profitable venture out of the gold, ivory, and slave trade there. By the 1890s, they had managed to conquer the entire territory and its Bantu population. Portugal by then was a declining power. Later, under the stultifying dictatorship of Antonio Salazar in the 1930s, it could invest little in its colony, except in the secret police. After the Second World War, Portugal began to export its unemployment by sending its own peasants out to develop the colony's tropical plantations. They, in turn, put the native Mozambicans into the hated forced-labour system. In 1961, to avoid UN interference in its colonial practices, Portugal turned all its colonies into "overseas provinces," making them part of the "mother country."

In 1962, some Mozambicans had had enough and formed the Mozambique Liberation Front (Frelimo), which two years later began an armed struggle against the Portuguese. This sporadic war went on for ten years against the same kind of brutal army repression publicized in the revolt of Angola, on the west coast of Africa. By 1974, when Frelimo controlled about one-quarter of sprawling Mozambique, the young Portuguese military captains themselves rebelled, formed the Armed Forces Movement, and overthrew the government in Portugal. They immediately negotiated a swift withdrawal from Mozambique, which became independent under Frelimo and its leader, Samora Machel, in 1975.

Some 250,000 white Portuguese settlers fled Mozambique to Portugal, to South Africa, and to Rhodesia, but not before destroying their cattle, wrecking their farm machinery, looting their factories, destroying records, and exporting illegally vast sums of money and crops. The new Frelimo government was faced with a bankrupt country bereft of trained doctors, engineers, and professionals, and with a populace whose illiteracy rate was over 90 per cent. Portugal's final legacy to Mozambique was an underdeveloped territory whose inhabitants spoke a dozen languages and had no sense of national identity.

Radicalized by a long war and inspired by Marxism, Samora Machel announced: "We do not recognize tribes, regions, race, or religious beliefs. We recognize only Mozambicans who are equally exploited and equally desirous of freedom and revolution."[2] He promised to make his country "the first fully Marxist state in Africa." And he did, by making Frelimo a Marxist-Leninist vanguard party and its policies the most collectivist in the continent. His somewhat grandiose promises of free universal health care, free universal education, public ownership, and equal sharing of the wealth were victims of a lack of infrastructure and good administrators, and of over-centralized planning. But above all, Mozambique was victimized by the war that was forced on the country in 1976.

A Strange and Obscene War

Mozambique's conflict did not begin as a civil war in the normal meaning of the term. The "rebels" were initially a few hundred black and white refugees from the colonial Portuguese forces gathered together by the intelligence organization of the white Rhodesian government. They were trained to return to Mozambique in 1976 to spy on and disrupt the activities of insurgents supporting Robert Mugabe, a leader of the Patriotic Front of Zimbabwe. These revolutionaries, with Frelimo's help, were using Mozambique as a base to attack Ian Smith's Rhodesian regime.

When Robert Mugabe's forces finally won control of Rhodesia/Zimbabwe in 1980, the rebel guerrillas turned to the South Africans for support. South African planes ferried these forces, now known as Renamo (the Mozambique National Resistance), to South Africa, where they were retrained, re-equipped, and bolstered with new recruits. Their new leader was Afonso Dhlakama, a Catholic-trained former soldier in the Portuguese army, who escaped from one of Frelimo's "re-education" camps. The rebels returned to Mozambique by land, by sea, and by air, and in 1981 intensified and expanded the guerrilla war throughout the country. Frelimo's army, now retrained as a conventional force by Soviet instructors, was inept and badly led, inadequate to the challenge.

Renamo became a useful part of South Africa's efforts to destabilize the so-called "frontline" African states nearby. Its first objective was to halt Frelimo's support for the African National Congress (ANC), the major anti-apartheid force, which was using Mozambique as a base to infiltrate its fighters into South Africa. Its second goal was to disrupt supply and trade routes in these neighbouring nations, most of which ran through Mozambique to the Indian Ocean. Finally, by wrecking Mozambique's economy and infrastructure, it would "prove" again that black majority rule did not work. The lesson at home was: South African apartheid must be accepted.

By 1984, Mozambique had lost control of three of four rail lines across the country, and nine of its ten provinces were in war zones. President Machel was forced to sign a non-aggression pact with South Africa, the Nkomati Accord, to close ANC bases in exchange for South Africa cutting its ties to Renamo. On top of the war damage, Mozambique had, in 1983-84, suffered through the worst drought outside Ethiopia; some 100,000 people died. But the brutal war, with no fixed fronts, few pitched battles, and an excess of terror, went on with South African help until, in 1986, Renamo almost managed to split the elongated country in two, driving to the coastal port of Quelimane.

The last remaining corridor, which contained a railway line, a highway, and an oil pipeline from the port city of Beira to Zimbabwe, was being kept open with the support of some 10,000 well-trained Zimbabwean troops, repaying Mugabe's debt to Frelimo. These troops began to help the Mozambican forces drive the Renamo guerrillas back into the more remote border areas in 1987, easing the pressure on the government.

The death of Machel in a plane crash in 1986 put Joaquim Chissano in charge. Slowly, the new government began to reassess its collectivist programs: state farms had been a failure; sending 50,000 urban unemployed out to farm had been a mistake; communal villages established to centralize services outran resources and became Renamo targets. With hardly any foreign investment coming in, Mozambique was becoming, like Bangladesh had been in the 1970s, a "basketcase."

What brought the international aid community flooding into Mozambique in 1987-88 was not just the obvious suffering but widespread reports of the vicious war being waged by Renamo, especially on children and non-combatants—a war in which 2 million people were turned into internal refugees, driven from their looted homes and facing starvation.

How Renamo Fights

Marie-Suzanne Prosper-DeBrouner, former UNICEF country representative in Mozambique, described in an interview what happens when a village is taken by Renamo: "They go into the village and they kidnap the women and young girls for two things. Because the women would grow the food, and the young girls would cook for them. Then they would rape them. By the time they are ready to leave, they either send them back or mutilate them. Sometimes they kill them. That is why I have no sympathy for them. As for the boys of the village, they take them away to train them as soldiers."

It could be worse. The Southern African Catholic Bishops Conference[3] reported that Renamo had been seen to boil children alive in front of their parents and had used the decapitated heads of old people as seats. The Southern Africa Research and Documentation Centre[4] in Zimbabwe reported that after kidnapping two girls from the Panda district in Inhambane province, they severely tortured them, cut off their lips and ears, and then gave them the severed organs saying: "Go and show these to your President."[5] Swedish Save the Children reported this: "The guerrillas gave Jose a rifle and told him to shoot down his father. At first Jose refused to do this and the guerrillas started to cut off his fingers with machetes. He lost four fingers before in desperation he shot his father. The guerrillas then forced him to join them as a soldier..." None of these reports was unique.

Aside from this savage terrorism, the Renamo guerrillas have won an infamous reputation for their wholesale scorched-earth policy. As William Finnegan reported in *The New Yorker* in a 1989 series on "The Emergency," the town of Morrumbala was picked as clean as vultures could strip a dead gazelle. "Every window, every window frame, every door, every doorframe, every piece of plumbing or wiring or flooring had been ripped out and carried away. Every piece of machinery that was well bolted down or was too heavy for a man to carry—water pumps, maize mills, the generator in the power station, the pumps outside the gas station—had been axed, shot, sledgehammered, stripped or burned." Houses, cars and trucks were burned. "There were few signs of battle—but a thousand signs of annihilative frenzy: each tile of a mosaic smashed, each pane of a glass-block wall painstakingly shattered. It was systematic, psychotically meticulous destruction."[6] Schools and health clinics were a special target all over Mozambique, along, of course, with their teachers and health workers. That is one reason why this country, along with Angola, has the highest under-five mortality rate in the world. But churches were usually saved, for, as Renamo leader Dhlakama has told the few journalists who have ever met him, he is for freedom of religion, free speech, free elections, and (at least in 1986) multi-party democracy.

Although recent revelations by former Renamo fighters allege that the South African Defence Force base at Phalaborwa, on the edge of Kruger National Park, running along the Mozambique border, is still a Renamo training ground, Dhlakama denies any South African links today. But Renamo had been receiving aid and financial support from Portugal, from ex-colonial Portuguese in Brazil and South Africa, and from right-wing groups in the United States.

Peace Talks But Little Peace

From 1990, Dhlakama and Mozambican representatives have been engaged in peace negotiations through a third party in Rome, the Catholic lay community of St. Egidio. As Felipe Mandlate, Secretary of State for Social Action in Mozambique, suggested during the conference, one reason for this development has been the 180-degree shift in policy of the Chissano government, which he described as "moving towards a free market economy." The government has also adopted multi-party democracy and promised to hold elections. The Chissano move caught Renamo off guard, taking away its ostensible purpose: the battle against Communism. It also forced Renamo's leader to consider multi-party elections. He was forced to talk, and as Mandlate said, agreements reached in the past two years had provided two "corridors of peace" in Mozambique, the old Beira one and a new one, running along the valley of the Limpopo river from Zimbabwe to the coast. But as he reminded delegates, they are not humanitarian but "economic corridors," required for transporting goods to landlocked Zimbabwe, and even these agreements have been breached by Renamo many times.

Meanwhile, the peace talks went on very slowly, with only 2 of the 16 points on the agenda yet settled as 1992 began. Renamo agreed to acknowledge Frelimo as the legitimate government, and Frelimo agreed to Renamo being recognized as a political party in the elections. But these conditions were to come into effect only when a cease-fire was achieved. Renamo continued to stall, hoping the government, which depended entirely on international aid to stave off collapse, would do just that. Renamo may also have needed time to organize a real political party.

While the Ottawa conference was in session, news came that Dhlakama had indicated he might agree to a Red Cross idea of establishing "zones of peace" in some areas, and the first he suggested was around the border town of Ressano Garcia on the main road to South Africa. President Chissano had earlier endorsed the concept.

During the working sessions, the idea of seeking humanitarian cease-fires in order to vaccinate children in war-torn regions of Mozambique was thoroughly discussed. Mandlate said that "since Renamo is not a political organization, it would be very difficult to work out an agreement for a humanitarian cease-fire with them," especially as he feared they would use it as grounds for military manoeuvres. Further, he said, it could "jeopardize the peace process." Mandlate reminded the working group that there were also tribal considerations involved. There are many tribal warlords around the country whose undisciplined forces raid villages and attack aid convoys. Furthermore, tribal Mozambicans live in homesteads rather than villages, and this makes delivering services, like health care, extraordinarily difficult. When UNICEF in 1985 tried a vaccination program in the country, it could not broadcast the fact by radio for fear of Renamo attacks. Some vaccination was achieved, with unprecedented difficulty, through Frelimo party cells by word of mouth. And in many remote regions the tribal people will not even go for immunization before checking with their local medicine man.

Mandlate felt that more might be accomplished through peace

education, perhaps through the churches and schools, to prepare the ground for such cease-fires. This could even lead in the long run towards conflict resolution, if the combatants were persuaded of the need for peaceful relations. The working group issued a statement at the end of the conference proposing that the Centre for Days of Peace help send a mission to Mozambique to assess the possibility of establishing an education for peace program with these aims. But as one experienced international aid official, who has met Dhlakama, observed during the conference, the need for immediate humanitarian aid is great now. "So if you want to work in hell, you have to talk to the devil. Why not talk to Renamo?"

In the spring of 1992, talks were not going well. The proposed "zone of peace" had not been implemented. Renamo seemed to be stalling again, the drought was becoming the worst in half a century, corruption was rampant even in government circles, and theft of aid at the Maputo docks was so bad some aid groups were threatening to pull out of Mozambique.

The terrible famine throughout Southern Africa was wasting all Mozambicans by mid-1992, however, and even the Renamo-held areas were seeking relief aid. Drought eventually drove both sides to the peace table. An agreement at the Rome talks was reached to permit delivery of food aid to rebel areas, so long as Mozambican troops did not accompany it. Then, in August, Renamo and Mozambique government leaders agreed to sign a cease-fire in October 1992.

It took some weeks to get the word around the war-ravaged country, so some fighting dragged on. Then, just before Christmas 1992, with cease-fire holding and the rains returning, the UN Security Council authorized a large UN military/civilian task force to oversee the implementation of the peace accord in 1993 and provide the badly needed aid. The first units of a planned 8000-man UN peacekeeping force were to arrive in January but were delayed by the more urgent UN attention to Somalia and Yugoslavia.

Despite hundreds of minefields and destroyed roads, food relief was being trucked into the countryside, even to Renamo areas, thousands of refugees were returning from neighbouring countries, and multi-party elections were being planned for 1994.

SRI LANKA

The "pearl of the Indian Ocean" was once a tropical island jewel of comparative religious peace and relative racial tranquillity. But Sri Lanka, the "Holy Ceylon" of old, is now an unholy killing ground for its peoples, an island of stunning beaches, of scrubby northern plains and jungle, and of vivid green, forested mountains, hiding racial hatred, religious animosity, and economic decline.

Since 1984 a civil war has been going on between the Sinhalese, who are mostly Buddhists and dominate the government, and the Tamils, the country's biggest minority, who are largely Hindus. It has been a bloody, guerrilla-type war, in which cease-fires are rare and erratic and hardly ever for humanitarian reasons.

The Historical Background

Four hundred and fifty years of Portuguese, Dutch, and British colonial rule had produced a tea and rubber economy in Ceylon. A well-educated, English-speaking elite were running the country when independence was granted without a rebellious note in 1948. The country appeared to be on its way to becoming a model developing nation, where Buddhists, Hindus, Muslims, and Christians would continue to live in relative harmony, as they had for centuries. Then some Sinhalese politicians sought to solidify their power by turning the majority in the population against a minority. The Tamils were to become their target.

There had been Tamils in the northern and eastern provinces of Ceylon for hundreds of years, the Ceylon Tamils. Then there were the Indian Tamils, the lowest caste Hindus brought over by the British in the 1840s to work in their coffee and tea plantations. To many Sinhalese, all Tamils were a threat. Just across the Palk Strait in India were 40 million Tamils casting a great shadow. According to Sinhalese politicians, Ceylon's Sinhalese majority was really a lonely minority in a South Asian sea of Tamils. Added to this paranoia was a legacy of envy. The British had encouraged Tamils to become civil administrators and to enter business, and they had prospered. Sinhalese felt the Tamils dominated government jobs and the professions.

The first move of the independent government in 1949 was to disenfranchise the Tamil tea-plantation workers. In 1956, Solomon Bandaranaike swept to power championing Sinhala Buddhism and Sinhalese as the national language. It was the 2,500th anniversary of Buddha's death and the "chosen people" were in power. There were anti-Tamil riots in 1958. A pact with India was signed in 1964 to send some 500,000 Tamil tea-workers back to India over a number of years.

In 1965, the chief parliamentary opposition party stole the government's agenda. With equal Buddhist zeal, with support from the politicized monks, and by refurbishing the legends of ancient Sinhalese kings, the United National Party took control of Ceylon in the election. The two major parties, both dominated by English-speaking elites, traded power back and forth over the next decade. In 1972 the nation became Sri Lanka, and their Tamil colleagues dropped away and formed their own party. Their first demand was for autonomy, then, in 1975, for a separate state in the north and east of the island. The Tamil United Liberation Front still held seats in parliament, but frustrated young Tamils were heading for the jungle. Sinhalese leaders in Colombo, the capital, could not seem to read the writing in the sand, and nothing much was done until 1983. Meanwhile, a siege mentality developed on each side.

During the summer of 1983, Tamil guerrillas ambushed and killed 13 soldiers. The army retaliated brutally and the Sinhalese community, unrestrained by its political leaders, went on a week-long rampage, burning Tamil shops, destroying Tamil homes, and killing hundreds of their fellow countrymen. The civil war had begun.

It soon became apparent that the most militant and best armed of the Tamil bands was the Liberation Tigers of Tamil Eelam

(LTTE), an implacably separatist faction. The Tigers, with training camps in friendly Tamil Nadu state, only an hour's ride by fast boat across the Palk Strait in India, were buying weapons there by milking cash from wealthy Sri Lankan Tamils. Based in Jaffna, the major Tamil town on a peninsula on the northern rim of the island, LTTE forces, which initially had been striking at police posts and army patrols, now struck back everywhere in the north and east. Their leader, a cunning fighter named Vellupillai Prabakaran, encouraged his men to ambush and massacre, executing innocent civilians by the busload and in remote villages. The Sri Lankan army, with three bases in the north, replied in kind, burning houses of Tiger suspects or picking up innocent Tamils and torturing them, forcing them to betray the location of Tiger hide-outs in the jungles.

"India could not remain silent," the late Indira Gandhi said when the first Tamils were massacred. Then, in 1987, her son Rajiv, who succeeded her as prime minister, put serious pressure on Sri Lankan President J.R. Jayewardene to halt the slaughter. It might have been seen as a cynical move by the leader of the country that had armed and trained the Tigers. But a pact was signed between the two countries and a 15,000-man Indian "peacekeeping" force was sent in to keep the sides apart and disarm the Tigers. The pact also forced Sri Lanka to concede that it was a multi-ethnic, multilingual state and called for political autonomy for the Tamil-dominated provinces.

To the concern of Sri Lankans, that Indian peacekeeping force grew to 50,000. Its fight with the six to seven thousand-man Tamil forces was embarrassingly inept and bloody, and the Tigers were never fully disarmed. The Indian peacekeepers finally left in 1990 with their mission unaccomplished and their reputation tarnished by their brutality.

The Tamil Tigers took over the northern and eastern countryside again. They massacred those Tamils who had collaborated with the Indians or who had abandoned the goal of independence, and attacked the Muslim Moors in the eastern provinces, as well as defenceless Sinhalese. The Sinhalese army, assisted by paramilitary forces, resumed its equally ruthless warfare. The trail of blood even led to India in 1991 when Rajiv Gandhi was assassinated, allegedly by some Tamil Tigers, in retaliation for the work of his peacekeepers. In the meantime, every effort by politicians or third parties to bring about a cease-fire resulted in failure. Rajiv's pact solved nothing.

In light of such a traumatic and often deadly situation, it was understandable that the people from all sides who attended the Ottawa conference did not want to be quoted. They did, however, provide a vivid description of the state of affairs in the war zones at the end of 1991, and the often remarkable efforts that have been made by local NGOs and others to provide humanitarian aid to the people caught in this tragic conflict.

In the northern province, the entire Jaffna peninsula was cut off by the Sri Lankan army and navy as 1992 began. The only main road to the south through Elephant Pass was closed to truck and other traffic. The Tamil Tigers ran Jaffna's administration, law and order, education and health services, and transport. The International Committee of the Red Cross, by agreement with the army, had established a neutral zone around the Jaffna hospital. But food and medicines were in short supply, prices had quintupled, and there hadn't been a phone service for four years.

The Sri Lankan government, less from humanitarian motives than those of duty, had for some time sent in food by ship to the docks at Point Pedro near Jaffna. Half of this went to the Tigers. But with the monsoon season, these supplies had to be shipped to an army base port further south, and re-shipped in amounts determined by the army.

The Sri Lankan NGOs have had the most experience in dealing with both the army and Tiger forces. They have maintained some channels of entry into Tamil sectors and provided aid to the children and families among the 300,000 refugees trapped in the Jaffna peninsula. This corridor was maintained not by any formal cease-fire, but by tacit agreement between the two sides.

In 1991, the Sri Lankan army, which had been engaged for the two years largely in quelling a bloody, left-wing Sinhalese peasant revolt in the south, returned in force to the eastern province, which had been badly hit by Tamil attacks the year before. It managed to establish some stability but only on the main roads and in the major towns. Some 135,000 displaced people still lived in refugee camps in the east and near Colombo. The Tamil Tiger forces now moved inland, living off the land and the local farmers, continuing their hit-and-run attacks and ambushes, with drastic effect on the local economy. Because of these conditions, local NGOs had difficulty reaching many isolated villages with aid. The mobile clinic that used to immunize children in remote areas had to be closed down when government aircraft bombed and killed two of its medical workers in their clearly marked vehicle. The government also used psychological warfare techniques in trying to pressure the Tamil guerrillas, even using the food relief as a weapon of war, a claim that is denied by authorities in Colombo.

It may be clear to outsiders, as it is to many moderate Sinhalese, Tamils, and others in the country, that the various Sri Lankan governments, dominated as they were by Sinhalese politicians, waited far too long to negotiate the serious concerns of their Tamil constituents, letting the pressure build to anger and to civil war. But in a country where Sinhalese citizens make up 74 per cent of the population and the Tamil populace only 18 per cent, how can this vicious war end in a peaceful settlement?

Unlike in El Salvador, there does not seem to be a religious mediator at hand. The Catholic church has members in both Tamil and Sinhalese communities, but neither the dominant Buddhist authorities nor the Hindu priests have shown any moderating influence on the warring parties, either through chauvinism on the one hand or fear on the other.

There seems to have been no concerted international pressure or plan by an international aid agency to bring about a humanitarian cease-fire, as in the Sudan. But the UN High Commissioner for Refugees did set a useful precedent by taking steps to protect internally displaced people in Sri Lanka.

A Parliamentary Road to Peace?

The only tiny flame of hope on the horizon in 1992 was the parliamentary action of an opposition Sinhalese member, Mangala Moonesinghe. A lawyer from the south, in 1987 Moonesinghe contested a seat in a constituency where armed Sinhalese insurgents opposed any vote. He won his seat for the Sri Lankan Freedom Party, the chief opposition. He believed, he said, that democracy, which had been eroded by the civil war, should prevail. He showed this by going to the legal defence of some of the Sinhalese insurgents charged with bombing parliament during the bloody two-year insurrection in 1988; they were acquitted.

Although, as he said, international pressure led to a brief cease-fire in 1990, allowing trains to run between Colombo and Jaffna and farmers in the north and east to start cultivating again, that cease-fire broke down after Indian forces left and negotiations failed. As a result of his experiences at mediation, he decided in 1991 that something more had to be done to bring the sides together. Moonesinghe noted that one party or the other, while in opposition, had managed for years to scuttle any government negotiations with the Tamils. As he said in an interview at the Ottawa conference: "I moved as a private member that we appoint a select committee of all the parties that are represented in parliament—Sinhalese, Muslims, Tamils—and that all sit and try to find a solution." His motion was supported by the government, by his own party, and by all the other parties. All felt this method might "at least provide the framework" for meeting members of the political wing of the Tamil Tigers. The mandate for the select committee was twofold. Its first set of goals was to establish permanent peace in Sri Lanka; to prevent the disintegration of Sri Lanka; to prevent further killing of civilians; to end the culture of violence and militarization; and to see that expenditures on military build-up are diverted towards development. The second goal was to develop a basic framework for the devolution and decentralization of government to the northern and eastern provinces.

As the committee began its work in 1992, it was hoped that the LTTE would support the process and that the international community would try to influence the Tiger supporters to accept conciliation. "I'm not optimistic at all," said Moonesinghe, "but neither am I wholly pessimistic, for we have taken one effective step towards conflict resolution."

Moonesinghe was interested in a suggestion from the conference's Sri Lanka working group that an agreement be sought to open Elephant Pass, the key road to Jaffna, one day a week as a symbol of goodwill—a move that might eventually help in the task of conflict resolution. But (as at this conference) there were no Tamil Tiger representatives coming forward for these discussions in Sri Lanka. Muslim representatives had already told Moonesinghe that they could not appear before his committee for fear the Tigers would kill them.

In late 1992, both sides insisted that they were abiding by the Geneva Conventions. The government promised to reform the army and has "accepted" 30 of Amnesty International's 32 recommendations on human rights. But even the idea of humanitarian cease-fires for Sri Lanka seemed remote, because the Tigers would not accept a "cease-fire" in the present circumstances for fear the army would take advantage of it. Since the army in its present siege of the Tamil north seems to feel it can only obtain communal peace by force, they may have a point. The bloodshed continues and parliamentary efforts at reconciliation have seemingly gone nowhere in 1992.

In such a delicate and dangerous situation, someone suggested, perhaps both sides might accept "creative humanitarian interventions" to help the children and non-combatants caught in Sri Lanka's nine-year civil war. Perhaps this fine semantic distinction might open the "corridors of communication" so badly needed if Sri Lanka is to provide more humanitarian assistance and a resolution of its poisonous conflict.

BURMA/MYANMAR

For over 30 years, the richly endowed country of Burma has been isolated from the world, not by its mountains but by the dictates of a military government indifferent to international opinion. It is a country that, as a result, has sunk to the status of one of the least developed nations of the world. It is also a country whose people have, by free and fair vote, overwhelmingly rejected the government of a general, Ne Win, who, though officially retired, still holds the reins of power.

Since its independence from the British in 1948, Burma has had to contend with a creeping civil war, taking place largely in the hill country around the central plains. This civil war was exacerbated by the spontaneous uprising of the people in 1988 and by the suppression of a democratically elected government voted in in opposition to the regime of General Ne Win. Thousands, especially young people, have fled to the hills to join the minority fighting groups. The result is a war with no front and no limits, and one that is especially dangerous for children given the Burmese army's refusal to abide by international standards for humanitarian rights.

In an irony of history, the long Burmese fight for independence is newly focused in the minds and actions of the Burmese people by the return to her homeland of Aung San Suu Kyi, the daughter of Burma's most respected leader of the democratic movement, Aung San. His aims for unifying the diverse peoples of Burma and his integrity in developing a democratic country, lost in the years of military authoritarianism, are being recalled by the people in the second revolution now under way in Burma.

The Historical Background

Burmese history recounts that a Burma the size and shape of the present country was united by force of arms by its own kings more than 900 years ago. After centuries of internal strife and invasion,

Burma's last king was ousted in 1885 by the British, who annexed the land to India. Using the usual divide-and-rule tactics, the British kept the hill tribes separated from the Burmese lowlands. Then the Japanese brought "co-prosperity" to Burma in 1942, the Japanese version of an economic empire allegedly to be shared with fellow Asians. Like many Asian colonials at that time, Aung San, a prominent student leader, joined others in seeking independence from Britain by accepting Japanese help. One of the so-called "Thirty Comrades" (who included General Ne Win), Aung San led a small Burma Independence Army into Rangoon alongside the Japanese invaders and drove out the British. But the Japanese promise of independence proved brutally hollow, and Aung San and his army joined the British in retaking the country in 1945.

By taking a tough stand with the British, Aung San forced negotiations for independence. He also held successful negotiations with some tribal groups—the Shans, Chins and Kachins—and agreed to unite the Burmese region with these tribal areas in a federal union. The constitution that he helped to draft made these tribal regions states within the Union of Burma and promised them local control of administration, language, and culture. Only the Karens, who were spread over wide areas of the south and who wanted an independent state, were not satisfied. Just when Aung San's dream of a democratic socialist state under a parliamentary system of government was within reach, he was assassinated in 1947 by a jealous rival.

The first decade of independent Burma turned out to be somewhat chaotic. Fighting the Communist underground and Karen rebels, the government of U Nu, Aung San's successor, was indecisive and inefficient, the army heavy-handed, its generals restless, and the economy sagging. General Ne Win was easily persuaded to take charge of a caretaker government for two years in 1958, during which time the Shan state rebelled. Returned to power, U Nu opted for making Burma a Buddhist state, which incensed the animist and Christian tribespeople.

In 1962, Ne Win led a military coup, abolished parliament, dissolved the high courts, absorbed the police into the military, put military officers in the governing Revolutionary Council and in top posts of most civil departments, and introduced the "Burmese Way to Socialism," which was to cut Burma off from most foreign influences. By then the Kachins were also in revolt, especially after Ne Win produced the 1974 constitution which said the Burmese land was one and inseparable and the minorities had no real control over their hill country and its resources. The deadening weight of military socialism left Burma a country at war and economically depressed, its greatest exports—teak, jade and opium—smuggled from the jungle outskirts, often with help from Ne Win's army officers. Its most important imports, from West Germany and other Western nations, were weapons of war.

Louisa Benson, a Karen representative with the Democratic Alliance of Burmans who attended the Ottawa conference, recounted what it was like in those days for the opposition. Her husband, a Karen brigade leader, was involved in prolonged peace talks with the Ne Win government in 1964. On one trip to Rangoon under "safe conduct," he failed to return, and she never found out how he died. The military tried to entice Louisa out of the Karen hills, because she was a film actress and the daughter of a wealthy, well-known Karen businessman. They even tortured her mother, who was in Rangoon. "It's that kind of government," she said.

Louisa joined the Karen military forces under General Bo Mya and worked at his headquarters in the Dawna Range on the Thai border. At 25 she was a liaison officer and a good shot with a carbine. She would track through the jungle with fellow guerrillas to link up with other Karen brigades, negotiate with top Thai officials to allow their troops to move inside the Thai border, or go on month-long campaigns in Karen territory against the Burmese army. As a prominent figurehead, Louisa gave pep talks to the troops and rallied the villagers, without whose help the Karen forces could not survive. When her family finally got out of Burma after two and a half years, she followed them to the United States.

People's Revolution
In the spring and summer of 1988, the repression of the Burmese people became intolerable. Spontaneous uprisings began, led by students and Buddhist monks. Hundreds of students were massacred, adding to the furore of the protests. Ne Win resigned. His military successor lasted only 18 days. A civilian successor then lasted less than a month. Aung San's daughter, Aung San Suu Kyi, was in Rangoon on a visit from England to see her dying mother. She became involved in the protest, and her presence ignited the crowds. Several hundred thousand attended her first speech before Rangoon's Shwedagon Pagoda, whose delicate golden spires crown Burma's most sacred site.

Three weeks later, direct military rule was imposed under the SLORC, the State Law and Order Restoration Council. It banned gatherings of more than four people, but at the same time allowed political parties to form for multi-party elections, as promised by Ne Win on his resignation.

The well-educated, well-travelled Aung San Suu Kyi is a believer in Mahatma Gandhi's non-violent civil disobedience methods. She urged non-violence on her followers as they began to campaign around the country for social change and democratic rights. She was so successful in exposing the government's human rights violations and encouraging people to call for democracy that on July 20, 1989, she was put under house arrest. Her movement, the National League for Democracy, nevertheless won an overwhelming electoral victory on May 20, 1990, taking 392 of 485 seats in the parliament. The SLORC party, which is still inspired by Ne Win from his mansion on Inya Lake in Rangoon, won only ten seats.

Since then, the SLORC government has ignored the election results, refused to call the assembly together, and has said it will not transfer power until a new constitution of its devising is written. Meanwhile, Aung San Suu Kyi, winner of the 1991 Nobel Peace Prize for her unflagging efforts to attain democracy, human rights, and ethnic conciliation by peaceful means, has been kept incommunicado in her house in the Burmese capital.

The Reverend Saboi Jum, a Baptist pastor and a Kachin who is head of the Burma Peace Committee, brought the conference up to date on recent happenings in Burma. He described how church leaders in Kachin state had tried in 1980 to bring Kachin insurgents and Ne Win together to halt the civil war. After six months' silence, Ne Win agreed to talks, and a brief cease-fire was achieved in the Kachin region. But the Burmese Communists, based in China, disliked this and sent a column of troops into Kachin to break the cease-fire. The war became more brutal. One time in 1986, Jum visited a Kachin village and "there were 37 women and children killed in a single day because they had been used as human minesweepers." In this case, the troops wanted to re-open a lead mine in which the insurgents had placed mines. They also seized young boys from villages, used them as porters to carry supplies, and forced them to walk ahead of troops to detonate guerrilla mines. He said the regime used the method of the four cuts: "They cut medicine, they cut food, they cut clothing, and they cut relationships. And so the children suffered."

Saboi Jum said security in the Rangoon area was tightened at the end of 1991 because of Karen attacks in the nearby delta region. In northern Burma, he said, the SLORC and the Chinese government were collaborating to build a four-lane highway between Kunming and Lashio, while the Chinese had helped the government gain control of another road in Kachin state that had been held by the rebel forces for 17 years. He said that some 100 villages, whose inhabitants had been linked with rebel forces, had been destroyed in June and July 1991. The people were removed to government relocation centres, resulting in the deaths of many children. This was happening in Kachin, Shan, and Karen states.

Louisa Benson, who has re-established contact with the Karens, reported that there were about 55,000 displaced persons on the Thai-Burma border, and that education for children was in local makeshift schools at the primary level only. There was a measles epidemic in Karen state, along with many cases of malaria, tuberculosis, and typhoid. Vaccinations for children were unknown in many regions of the state.

Another member of the conference working group, Allison Tate, an Australian who worked with Burmese students who fled their country after the 1988 uprising, reported that female students who ended up at the immigration detention centre in Bangkok were often beaten or sexually abused. Young teenage girls were offered work near the Thai border, then rounded up by the military and sold to brothels in Chiang Mai and Bangkok. Many who sought protection under the UN High Commissioner for Refugees found that office could not protect them if the Thai authorities did not co-operate.

Humanitarianism Rejected

Although the outside world, after the 1988 uprisings, changed its perceptions of what the SLORC now calls Myanmar, the men from the SLORC only hardened their attitudes. Having arrested most of the leaders of the National League for Democracy, giving some elected members 25-year jail terms, the regime began to root out lower-level suspects. All civil servants had to answer a list of leading questions to expose their alleged disloyalty to the SLORC. Saboi Jum said some 15,000 were fired as a result.

The army's growing campaign against the opposition in the hills was aided by the collapse of the Burmese Communist forces. China's participation in a billion dollar weapons deal with the Myanmar government is changing the shape of the civil war. Embargoes the West placed on arms sales in 1988 were soon broken by Singapore, Pakistan, Poland, and also the disintegrating

Soviet Union. So the Burmese army continues in business. A new public holding company, set up in 1990, ensures that the army is well financed for more arms deals, probably through military control of the lucrative heroin trade.

Despite all this, the Ottawa conference working group thought humanitarian cease-fires to help the children might be possible. Some areas were still under tribal control, and donor organizations could provide assistance like immunization without a countrywide cease-fire. But an international organization like UNICEF would be needed to negotiate with the government and opposition forces in order to achieve any humanitarian cease-fire.

Murray Thomson, who has lived and worked in neighbouring Thailand and who now heads Canadian Friends of Burma, told the working group that the opposition to the SLORC had begun to coalesce recently. The tribal minorities have already renounced their demand for independent states outside the Union of Burma and allied with the pro-democracy Burmese in a truly national war of liberation. They formed the National Coalition Government of the Union of Burma (NCGUB), which includes a number of members elected in 1990 from Aung San's party who had escaped the SLORC's roundup and arrest of its leaders. This alternate government, including legitimately elected members, has the backing of the Democratic Alliance of Burmans and minorities, and is the only true government of Burma, the working group stressed. It considered that, although Burma had accepted the UN Declaration of Human Rights, the SLORC was one of the worst violators of those rights in the world. The working group called upon all parties in the conflict to halt human rights violations, "especially the use of children as human shields and forced labour." Finally, it agreed that the military junta should be called upon to respect the will of the people of Burma in their election of 1990 and to release Aung San Suu Kyi and all political prisoners. These were essential steps to end the conflict and ensure the future well-being of Burma's children.

As 1992 ended, the SLORC regime in Burma continued to be indifferent to international pressure. Its army expanded the terror campaign to the Muslim people of the Arakan region, driving some 200,000 of them into exile in Bangladesh. It began a major drive against the Karen people and tried to capture the headquarters of the NCGUB pro-democracy coalition in Manerplaw on the Thai border. Throughout the country, according to an Asian human rights report, there were more than a million internal refugees.

The country's dire economic state since 1988 caused the government to open up its resources to foreign investment for the first time in decades. American and Japanese investors rushed in, as did Petro-Canada, which has since withdrawn. As a result, Burma avoided bankruptcy and the SLORC regime was enabled to continue the tragic civil war. This financing of oppression, along with the increased world arms-trading with a nation at war against its own people, were issues, the group thought, that should be of concern to a United Nations currently debating how to control the arms trade and how to defend human rights and enlarge humanitarian assistance.

THE PHILIPPINES

The power of the people, of women and children, of nuns and working men, when they spontaneously join together to oust a dictator is probably the most vivid recent picture called to mind when we think of the Philippines. When they rejected Ferdinand Marcos, elected Corazon Aquino, then took to the streets to ensure her elevation to the presidency, the people proved that if they acted together in a righteous cause they could make history. Those four days of revolution in 1986 were tense yet relatively tolerant. The people jammed the Manila streets defying the troops and halting the tanks. They were taunting and smiling not shooting, until finally the ailing autocrat Marcos, his first lady, and their flunkies were flown away by the Americans who had helped to keep him in power for 13 years.

Some Filipino people have also shown that if those at the bottom of the ladder stand up to aggression, they can achieve, in a somewhat different fashion, the kind of respite from civil war for humanitarian purposes that took place in El Salvador and the Sudan.

The Historical Background
Called by Americans, "the showcase of democracy," the Philippines had a history of colonial rule and peasant repression even before Marcos declared martial law in 1972 and ruled its 7,107 islands as an avaricious dictator. For over three hundred years it was a colony of Spain, whose legacy was Roman Catholicism and forced labour on sugar and tobacco plantations. When the people rebelled against Spain in the 1890s, the Americans sought their Manifest Destiny there and in Cuba by intervening. But instead of freeing the Filipinos, they fought them for three years in a brutal war. In the ensuing state of democratic colonialism, a legislature was established and health services, mass education, and the infrastructure of a modern state were developed. Before the people of the Philippines

obtained independence in 1946, however, they were also subject to a ruthless occupation by the Japanese during the Second World War. Even after independence, the legacy of American rule and continued American economic domination was imposed upon a base of powerful, wealthy, landed families who held sway over the poor urban and peasant people. And it was no help that Washington had made this strategically located nation the home for two of its biggest military bases in the Pacific.

The Marcos dictatorship, spurred on by the covetousness of his wife Imelda, the "Steel Butterfly," only aggravated the resentment of the ordinary Filipino. A moderate senator, Leticia Ramos-Shahini, said: "Ours is a sick nation, gravely afflicted with the interlocking diseases of poverty, passivity, graft and corruption, exploitative patronage, factionalism, political instability, love of intrigue, lack of discipline, lack of patriotism, and a desire for instant self-gratification."[7] It is little wonder that the Filipinos eventually began to resent this foreign domination and the attendant domestic political corruption.

The first popular reaction to the corrupt way of life in the islands was the Huk rebellion in the 1950s, which was extinguished by the military. On Mindanao Island a 1970 uprising by the Muslim minority started the isolated rebellion of the Moro National Liberation Front that has dragged on for years. But in 1968 a band of student activists, led by a Maoist professor, headed for the countryside to stir up a national peasant revolution under the flag of the Communist Party of the Philippines. They formed the New People's Army (NPA). Although it was a minuscule presence when Marcos used it as an excuse for imposing martial law in 1972, the NPA grew in size and importance during his dictatorship. After world prices for coconuts plunged in the late 1970s and Corazon Aquino's husband, the popular Benigno, Marcos's chief political rival, was publicly murdered, civil war spread widely among the islands, and the armed forces of the Philippines reacted.

At first the NPA worked with the peasants, tried to defend them against cruel landlords, and even dispensed justice. But the army would come in and arrest barrio leaders for assisting the rebels. They burned down houses and destroyed crops in order to drive out the guerrillas. Eventually the NPA began to reply in kind, accusing village chiefs of being army informants and killing such "traitors."

Ed Garcia, a widely known peace activist and professor of political science at the University of Manila, told the Ottawa conference in emotive terms what this civil war had developed into by the time "Cory" Aquino came to power.

"In the Philippines, one of the tragic consequences of the protracted armed conflict is that the reasons why people took up arms in the first place were oftentimes overshadowed by the so-called 'blood debts' which the totality of the war engenders. When this stage is set then all hell breaks loose. Paramilitary forces are formed, as well as vigilante-type groups, which somehow privatize the war. Young people, some of them in their early teens, are recruited to fight on either side. Children grow up without enjoying their childhood, thus replicating the violence."

As someone who helped draft the 1987 constitution of the Philippines for the Aquino government, Garcia admitted that "we squandered an historic opportunity for laying the foundations for a lasting peace when we drove away a tyrant in 1986. What we began we could not sustain; we could not realize the aspirations of a people grown weary of war."

But lately "the guns of war were stilled by the wrath of nature." In the period between July 1990 and October 1991, the Philippines was in turn struck by a huge earthquake, the volcanic explosion of Mt. Pinatubo, and floods on Leyte Island that killed more than 8,000 people. In each case, short-lived humanitarian cease-fires were agreed to by the army and the NPA in order to rescue people and aid the injured. An unexpected positive result was that the volcanic disaster finally persuaded the Americans to agree to close both of their military bases and move away.

Grassroot Zones of Life

A more interesting and unusual development during this time was the grassroots establishment of "zones of life" in some of the war zones. Professor Garcia was most enthusiastic about this and what has flowed from it for the peace movement in the Philippines.

He explained, from his own background, how he learned the need for the empowerment of oppressed peoples. "As a young man I watched Manila shantytowns being demolished and the poor moved to the country, far from their workplaces. I heard from migrant sugar workers in Negros Occidental how they were harassed by their landlords." After watching the death and chaos created by the private armies of wealthy families in the early 1970s in Manila, he went to work in Latin America, where oppression of the poor was also rife. He joined Amnesty International. Back in the Philippines in the 1980s, he joined the noted civil rights champion Jose Diokno in working to develop people's movements, and the Ecumenical Commission for Displaced Families, a broad-based Christian organization that helps those in need of housing.

Many Catholic priests had become sympathetic to the plight of the peasants: some even joined the NPA. The Catholic church was instrumental in initiating cease-fires in connection with religious observances, such as during the Feast of Our Lady of Penafrancia in Naga City, or during Holy Week or Christmas elsewhere. In a largely Catholic country these were relatively easy to promote, but they proved to be of little use as humanitarian aid to children and noncombatants caught in widespread civil conflict.

Garcia has written: "Rights enshrined in international covenants or in our constitution at times are not enjoyed by many among our people.... People's power, therefore, does not only mean stopping tanks or toppling tyrants; more often it means working quietly together to enforce our basic rights: to food, shelter, and clothing; to work and to organize."[8]

That is exactly what the people in Cantomanyog, on the island province of Negros Occidental, decided to do in the mid-1980s. They were tired of harassment by the army and private vigilante groups hired by sugar planters, and they were equally tired of hit-and-run counter-harassment of NPA guerrillas, with their mobile patrols. The people got together, declared their community a "zone of peace," and called for the banning of military activities in the area. Then they contacted the military leaders and the NPA chiefs and worked to obtain their agreement.

There have been six such peace zones declared in rural areas over the past three years, Garcia said. Among these communities, or *barangays*, were Sagada in the Cordillera Central mountain area of northern Luzon Island; the Bituan "Zone of Life" in Tulunan, North Cotobato; the Tabuk "Matagoan Zone of Life" in Kalinga-Apayao; as well as Naga City in Camarines Sur.

The decisions of these communities to declare themselves demilitarized and weapons-free were not without problems. "Our experience is that cease-fires, no matter how limited, including humanitarian cease-fires, are difficult to initiate and implement, not only because they are highly susceptible to sabotage or failure, but also because their return to the status quo ante is seen by more and more people — especially the majority of victims, children — as simply unacceptable," Garcia said. The conflicts and negotiations were complicated by actions of the army, which encouraged spies in villages, impressed young boys into the military, imposed free-fire zones, and conducted a program of "hamleting," or the forced removal of villagers to government-run hamlets. At the same time, it was not in the interests of the NPA, which depended on villages for shelter and food, to assist them to become demilitarized "zones of peace."

Risa Baraquel, secretary-general of the Coalition for Peace of

Quezon City, told a conference working group that the political wing of the NPA, the National Democratic Front, often argued that "in many areas you can't separate us from the people because we are the only line of defence against social injustice and oppression." But she said the people in these peace zones, who have supported the rebels and even have children in both armies, are saying, "Even if ideologically we are kindred spirits, we cannot sustain the war effort any more. If soldiers or NPA fighters come to our house, we can't afford any more to feed them because times are harder and we just don't have the resources to sustain armies. We can't afford any more to send our children into armies. We want them to be with us, to finish their schooling, to work on the farms."

They now are saying to the combatants, including the NPA who are highly motivated, "We are just choosing a different way to advance the same issues, to make the same gains, through a different strategy.... The people caught in the middle want the war to stop. They can't afford the high cost of achieving political equality through armed struggle. They seek a third way, a middle way." So, she concluded, the negotiations for "zones of life" or "zones of peace" depend on the strength of the villagers' commitment to non-violence. This astonished a Salvadoran delegate present at the conference, who said in his country, and this was before the recent peace accord, the people working for the aims of social justice were committed to the armed struggle.

Building a Peace Plan

"Zones of life" were, however, only a first step, according to Garcia. The next stage involved building a common agenda or peace plan for a peaceful and productive life. The news of these cease-fires spread through local non-government aid organizations, the church, and the people. They became part of a Coalition for Peace that provided support services for communities, advocacy help, and psychosocial therapy for children. Studies showed that 50 per cent of civilian victims of the war were children, and that half a million Filipino children have been separated from parents or orphaned by the conflict.

It is not incidental that the constitution Garcia helped draft recognized for the first time as a right the role of people's organizations in constructing a just society. NGOs and other support groups for the poor could no longer be considered "subversive" or Communist. Multi-sectoral Peace Advocates appeared on the Philippine scene (Garcia is one) who could discuss the issues at the national level with both the government and the National Democratic Front. For, he said, even if there is no cease-fire, "we must encourage attempts to negotiate peace or a political settlement." And humanitarian cease-fires, he said, must be placed in the framework of peacebuilding: "For humanitarian action to have the maximum impact, it cannot be totally divorced from the peace process." In the Philippines, this also means encouraging peace education for all, from the young to the old.

"Cultural violence encourages violence to resolve problems, and that only helps the powerful," Garcia argued. Since governments act too little, too late, and too slowly on questions of peace, a National Peace Conference was convened in 1990. Then, in 1991, Multi-sectoral Peace Advocates produced for consideration by all parties a framework for a peace process agenda for the whole country. It covered social justice, the rights of indigenous peoples (like the Muslim Moros fighting for autonomy in the south), ecological problems, peace zones, social and cultural reforms, and moral transformation.

President Aquino stepped down in 1992, having survived seven right-wing military coups. Her chosen successor, Fidel Ramos, won election as president and pledged to seek an end to the 24-year war with the NPA. In the fall of 1992, he set up an "exploratory" meeting in the Netherlands between top government officials and Communist leaders. It produced a blueprint for, as news reports put it, "an overhaul of the country that would take into account human rights, social, economic, political, and constitutional reforms, and a way of re-integrating the insurgents into mainstream life." If these negotiations fail, the national agenda for peace and the inspiration of the "zones of life" may still provide a parallel peace process for the Philippines.

COLOMBIA

Reading the headlines, one might be excused for thinking that democracy in Colombia is dying from an overdose of drugs. The publicity garnered by U.S. President George Bush's 1989 "war on drugs," in which Latin America's third most populous country was a major target, tended to obscure the real war in this large and troubled democracy.

When Colombia attracts the attention of the Western media, it is to highlight assassinations, kidnappings, and the defiance of legal authority by the super-wealthy cocaine barons of Medellin. The longer-running, more persistent war of guerrilla forces in this Andean nation has had a much lower news profile. And the surprising actions of some of the peasants who are caught in the middle of these conflicts are rarely heard of outside Colombia.

The Historical Background

The roots of Colombia's civil disturbances go back to the beginnings of the nation's tenuous yet tenacious democratic institutions. After years of civil wars and violence in the nineteenth century, in 1903 the country saw its elite upper class settle down into a political system that featured a Conservative and a Liberal party. In the early 1940s there was a turbulent and bloody period, labelled *La Violencia*, which ended only when a pact was made to alternate parties in power. Aside from a brief five-year military interregnum in 1953-58, this oligarchic democratic system has lasted to this day. The two parties have even shared power in each other's cabinets and divided up the spoils of government. It has been called "consociational democracy" by scholars, or rule by the rich and their *caciques* (political bosses) by ordinary Colombians. In a predominantly Hispanic culture, closely aligned to the most conservative Catholic church in Latin America, this is a recipe for oppression and polarization: coffee plantation owners and cocaine processors get richer while the peasantry continues poor and harassed.

While Catholic priests in other parts of Latin America were growing restless about the poverty and social injustice faced by the peasantry, in Colombia religious reaction stood fast, despite rural violence in the 1940s in which some 200,000 died. Yet, ironically, it was in Medellin, Colombia, in 1968, at the council of Latin American bishops, that the "theology of liberation" was first enunciated, the revolutionary idea that the church ought to participate in educating the poor on their civil rights and the non-violent ways to achieve them. Colombia's bishop was the lone opponent to this new idea. Even in 1979 at the great Puebla conference of the church, addressed by Pope John Paul II, Colombia's pugnacious Archbishop Lopez Trujillo fought a losing battle against the church's continuing commitment to social justice and liberation.

Meanwhile, the principal guerrilla band, called the Colombian Revolutionary Armed Forces (or FARC), continued to grow in poverty-stricken Caqueta province and in the central Magdalena River valley. This offspring of the Communist party was challenged in 1970 by the M-19 band, romantic leftists and nationalists who opposed the establishment with highly publicized actions, like kidnappings and the capture of the Dominican embassy. Colombia's armed forces reacted by persuading the oligarchs to pass laws increasing their power and authorizing paramilitary forces to harass the guerrilla hide-outs. When Conservative populist Belisario Betancur was elected in 1982 and tried to offer an amnesty to the M-19 and reforms to the homeless, the amnesty was sabotaged by the army and the reforms were watered down or just killed by entrenched politicians.

By the mid-1980s there were seven different guerrilla bands operating not only in the mountains but in urban areas. With the growth of the cocaine trade, it is estimated that 137 paramilitary groups developed, some assisting the military and some carrying out the vindictive orders of the drug overlords. The most spectacular guerrilla attack was M-19's occupation of the Palace of Justice in

1985, and the killing of half the justices of the Supreme Court during the army's bloody recapture of this symbol of legality.

According to Penny Lernoux of Bogota,[9] a veteran writer on Colombian affairs, several thousand Colombians were assassinated in 1986 out of a nation of 28 million as part of the country's "dirty war." Amnesty International reported then that Colombia had become one of the worst violators of human rights in the hemisphere.

This explosive mixture of rebellion and repression, arms and money, poverty and obscene wealth created a chaotic picture. Carlos Montoya, a 30-year-old Bogota lawyer and member of the Communitarian Peace Foundation, said in a conference interview that "at the beginning, in the 1960s, the guerrillas had a very high political commitment and all their actions were to that end. But really they have become another part of common crime...." He recalled how in the 1970s, when oil was discovered and rich foreign oil companies came to exploit it, "the guerrillas found a source to finance their operations. By kidnapping oil executives and by extortion they got a lot of money. Some companies even offered them the arms they needed."

When the cocaine trade began to grow, he said, "the guerrillas found another source of money. They made deals with the coca dealers, saying 'We will look after your plantations, not report them to the government, but for a very high price.' Some even got involved in the [drug] trade by the 1980s." According to other observers, some FARC bands in certain areas have helped the coca growers by acting as an armed trade union, forcing the narco-dealers to pay proper wages and decent prices for the crops.

The U.S. government under Ronald Reagan preferred the idea that drugs and terrorism were linked to Communist guerrillas, since that theory supported its general strategy in Latin America. In the late 1980s, when the drug barons had become so well armed and so wealthy that they arrogantly offered to pay off the government's national debt, the government of Virgilio Barco had to turn to Washington for help. Then, in 1989, President George Bush unleashed his "war on drugs." Ignoring the demand side of the equation at home, Bush was now sending military aid that helped intensify both the drug war and the guerrilla war.

According to Montoya, there are today about 90 fronts around the country where the FARC is fighting. In each area the guerrillas face different circumstances, operate from different motives. Yet the fight is less about ideological issues now, and more over resources—oil, emeralds, gold, or land that wealthy guerrilla groups have purchased legally, often for local politicians whom they have decided to support. The result has been a love-hate relationship among the peasants, the guerrillas, and the armed forces.

Zone of Peace

In the midst of all this, in 1987, some peasants in the area of La India got fed up and called a halt to conflict. Carlos Montoya has described La India as "a peasant community, located in a jungle area along the Magdalena River in central Colombia." The main town in this colonization region is Cimitarra. When the FARC guerrillas came to hide out in this jungle area, they did an excellent job with the community, helping with health care and education. They were the "alternative government."

"In 1973 when the region had become a stronghold for FARC," Montoya said, "the army came in to evict the guerrillas. From then on life became a nightmare for the local population. The peasants were being killed and tortured by both the army and the guerrillas. The peasants were systematically accused by both sides of being 'informants' and 'supporters' of the enemy. In the early 1980s, the situation worsened when paramilitary groups came in, working either for the army or local politicians."

Twenty years after the peasants first settled this area, in May 1987, an army officer and paramilitary commanders summoned the peasants of La India to a meeting. As Montoya said, "They told the people they had three options from then on. The first one was to leave. The second one was to join one of the armed groups. And the third one was to stay and die.

"After that, two of the men, Hector Pineros and Josue Vargas, thought there must be a fourth option. So they went to talk to each of the armed groups and asked them one simple question: 'Who are you fighting for?' And everyone would respond, 'For you!' Then the peasants said, 'Okay, you have been fighting for us for ten or twenty years, but the main victims of these conflicts have been us. So we don't want you to fight on our behalf any more. We prefer to stay and work peacefully.'"

Several meetings were held. The peasants told the guerrilla commanders that their arbitrary killings had to stop, listing the names of those murdered and the killers. A list of conditions was also drawn up. First was the peasants' refusal to accept any more killings or torture. The second was that the peasants' obligation to provide food, lodging, or transportation must cease, unless the individual peasant wished to help. Third, the peasants should no longer be summoned to meetings to be accused of treachery or being an informant. Fourth, the peasants would not obstruct or denounce actions of the armed groups so long as they were not adverse to the peasants.

Similar meetings were held between peasants and the military and paramilitary groups, and a similar list of conditions was agreed to by them. Meetings grew in size until there were 5,000 peasants at a final session in July. The agreements covered a peasant population of about 7,000 and an area of 30,000 square kilometres of a district known as El Carare, of which La India is a part. The peasants also formed an Association of the Peasant Workers of El Carare (ATCC) to expand the peace process.

This grassroots-organized "zone of peace" has been a great success, though not without its problems. Since May 21, 1987, there have been no battles or tortures of peasants in La India. "The criminal law of silence" has been abolished, so peasants are not afraid to speak out and organize their lives. They have been working on their own economic and social development plan, and they have opened their own grocery store, bought two motorized canoes for their transport service, and purchased agricultural machinery. A six-year development plan was presented to the state institution for national rehabilitation.

Meanwhile, Carlos Montoya, who acted as adviser on human rights to President Barco, received 28 letters from local communities around Colombia exposing human rights violations but also calling for local peace talks. But the president's staff insisted only national cease-fire talks with all groups could be encouraged. So Montoya left to join the peace foundation, travelled to La India, and then got the 28 communities in touch with the ATCC organization to exchange information and experience. The foundation has been active in encouraging four communities to pursue this idea, while the other 24 are still considering the process.

The publicity that the peace zone in La India aroused in the Colombian media began to disturb the political bosses, and many leaders of the ATCC peasant association were being threatened for going too far too fast. Tension was high as a large peace forum was held in 1990 that set out new programs. Possibly as a result, in February 1990 Josue Vargas and two other ATCC leaders were assassinated in Cimitarra. That ugly gesture of intimidation was "a big setback," according to Montoya, and it encouraged the people in La India to recognize that the process would be a long one and had to be developed at a slower pace. But they agreed that they must continue the work, continue to dialogue with their opponents, and maintain the non-violent struggle for peace.

Montoya said that to propose this kind of cease-fire in these circumstances "requires more courage than fighting." The people of La India now are using the written story of their peace process as a way to teach their children, who have been damaged by the life of violence, to read and thus to receive a peace education. This do-it-yourself campaign had a message. As Montoya has said: "By creating your own way out, people gain incredible power. They are finding themselves, they find their own identity, and gain the respect of others." He also noted that people must be aware that "humanitarian actions have political consequences."

As 1993 began, insurgency was still a fact of life in Colombia. The war on drugs had not been won. Neither negotiating with the drug barons nor cracking down on them had been successful. In the struggle for peace, however, many of the political demands of guerrillas had been met. Direct election of mayors and governors, a lifting of the state of siege, appointment of a civilian defence minister, a constitutional convention, disarming of right-wing death squads, and the participation of M-19 guerrillas and Indians in the Congress had been achieved. Yet the best-armed guerrillas, FARC, were demanding new economic terms covering unemployment, taxes, high rents, hunger, and the high cost of food, water, education, and health care. But in November 1992, after guerrillas had dynamited the main oil pipelines for the fortieth time that year and massacred police at a major jungle oil installation, a national emergency was again declared. A cease-fire was still in the distance, after 30 years of conflict.

On an optimistic note, reporting on the spread of grassroots cease-fires, Montoya was able to tell his working group that, as a result of the Ottawa conference and his meetings with Ed Garcia, La India and Naga City in the Philippines have been twinned and will share their experiences in the future.

YUGOSLAVIA

Most of the case histories of conflict that have been discussed in this book have involved Third World countries, where the legacy of colonialism and a history of ethnic struggles have left their ugly marks in the civil wars of today. But the removal of the dying hand of Communism from the peoples of Eastern Europe and the lands of the old Russian empire have exposed ethnic and cultural cancers that grew more virulent and deadly the longer they were unattended. The continuing battles between Armenia and Azerbaijan over the mountainous, dislocated enclave of Nagorno-Karabakh is one nasty example. The civil war in Yugoslavia, the bloodiest in Europe since the Second World War, is another and more dangerous one.

The death of the Yugoslav federation was caused in part by the collapse of Communism in Eastern Europe and by the re-emergence of historic ethnic and cultural enmities. But it was deliberately exacerbated by the insensitive actions of the Serbian and Croatian leaders, and the ruthless methods of the Serbian-led Yugoslav national army and Serb and Croat irregular forces.

The Historical Background

This South Slav state came into being in 1918 as the Kingdom of the Serbs, Croats, and Slovenes and was called Yugoslavia in 1929. The Serbian king treated the other regions as annexed, which outraged some Croats.

The Croats formed a terrorist society, Ustasha, that collaborated with Nazi Germans. In 1941 they declared Croatia independent. Some Serbs in Croatia formed a group called the Chetniks to fight the German invader. But Marshal Tito, a Croatian Communist, rallied followers with a more internationalist ideology. He drove out the Germans and established an authoritarian federation that brought together Serbs, Croats, Slovenes, as well as Montenegrans,

Macedonians, the people of Bosnia and Herzegovina, and Albanians and Magyars in two autonomous regions. His moderate if idiosyncratic communism, which allowed Tito to break with the Soviet bloc in 1948, persisted until 1990.

After Tito's death in 1980, the collective presidency that ran the country allowed the diverse nationalisms to reassert themselves. Then in 1989 Communist regimes began to fall in all of Eastern Europe. The surrounding break-up inevitably affected Yugoslavia. Slobodan Milosevic, the leader of the most populous republic, Serbia, asserted Serbian authority over the Albanian Kossovo region and continued to defend a Communist-style federalism. But in Slovenia and Croatia the drive for autonomy became one for separation, and in 1991 both republics declared their independence and were recognized by the outside world.

Croatia's leader, Franjo Tudjman, an ex-Communist, set out to nationalize his territory and make it a separate country for the Croats, even though Serbs had lived peacefully with Croats for years. In Serbia, irregular forces of Serbian nationalists, with the assistance of the Serbian-led Yugoslav national army, took it upon themselves to liberate their fellow Serbs who were being treated so contemptuously by Tudjman's police and militia. Civil war of the most brutal kind exploded, and most of it was fought in the towns and villages of Croatia. The devastating artillery and aerial bombardment of civilians by the army, and the house-to-house killing and terrorism in these towns by irregular forces, was televised to a shocked Europe. The siege of Vukovar was just the first, most publicized example.

A Flawed Aid Mission

How to reach women and children trapped in the cellars of these devastated places, or to remove the wounded from bombed-out hospitals, were two of the problems facing aid organizations in this situation. Two members of Médecins sans Frontières (MSF), Jacques de Milliano and Françoise Bouchet-Saulnier, told the conference what it was like, and what the obstacles to a humanitarian cease-fire can be.

Although 14 cease-fires were attempted, usually through European Economic Community (EEC) intervention, Bouchet-Saulnier said at that time there had "actually been one effective humanitarian cease-fire in Yugoslavia, negotiated by Médecins sans Frontières, which evacuated wounded people from the besieged hospital in Vukovar." The other cease-fires, aimed at obtaining a truce in the combat, were generally violated. The European Community tried to achieve cease-fires to allow negotiations for peace and for food convoys to besieged towns, but nearly all failed.

Bouchet-Saulnier said MSF was especially concerned about the wounded in Vukovar hospital."It was completely destroyed, although wounded were in the basement. The situation was very, very bad, so we decided, on a humanitarian basis, to organize what we call a sanitary medical evacuation, which is embodied in the Geneva Conventions. We asked for this right to evacuate the wounded and we were not willing to bring into the city any relief. We had a lot of trouble to get this idea across to the federal mind, the Croatian mind, and Serbian mind. Even the EEC mind wanted to deal something else besides. Then we managed, mainly through broadcasting on Serbian and Croatian radio, to have this idea spread about, insisting that the word 'humanitarian' must precede the word about the convoy. It took us all day, going every half hour to the broadcasting studio to insist our communique be read in full." Apparently the radio people kept saying it was a convoy negotiated by the military, and it was hard to get across the simple idea of humanitarianism.

The MSF people loaded up their convoy of 10 trucks, and with the minefields on the road cleared they had no trouble reaching Vukovar. They had no choice of route and were forced to cross five front lines and two no-man's-lands over a distance of 15 kilometres. "We loaded 109 wounded persons on trucks and ambulances, and then on the way back we hit a mine, despite the clearance." Two nurses were wounded, and the army forced the convoy to leave the main road and take a muddy and extended route through Serbia to get back to their Croatian base. It took 24 hours to cover what should have been 20 kilometres.

Then the MSF team discovered that their humanitarian convoy and humanitarian cease-fire had been linked to a military action. As de Milliano said, in order to get medical supplies needed for the convoy, MSF had to negotiate with the European Community. Its political officials had linked the MSF operation to the efforts of the Serbian army to end the Croatian blockade of their Zagreb barracks, so its soldiers could be released and returned to Serbia. To an NGO like Médecins sans Frontières, this action meant its cherished neutrality and independence had been compromised.

Bouchet-Saulnier noted that MSF and the International Committee of the Red Cross later "engaged in negotiating a new cease-fire with the federal and Croatian authorities to finish the evacuation of the Vukovar hospital. But it became apparent afterwards that these negotiations were being used by the military authorities as a delaying tactic. The agreement was only finalized after the fall of the city, by which time the evacuation of the wounded and civilians had already been largely carried out behind Serbian lines without humanitarian control."

This use of humanitarian cease-fires for political or military purposes was widely discussed in the conference workshops and deplored by aid groups. James Grant, the head of UNICEF, told those attending the conference that "Yugoslavia is on everyone's agenda. The aborted attempt to get a corridor into Vukovar represents a failure of the international community. But in contrast, the water corridor to Dubrovnik represents a success. Once again ICRC and UNICEF collaborated on this initiative, with the backing of the European Economic Community."

"Water Corridor of Peace"

The bombing of the beautiful old port of Dubrovnik had gone on for several weeks, and relief teams on ships outside the harbour could not get past the naval vessels blockading the city. What eventually happened was the initiation of the first "water corridor of peace" for the landing of relief supplies for children. In an interview, Staffan DeMestura, a UNICEF deputy director who helped organize the corridor, said that "Dubrovnik had been under siege from October 1 to November 14, by which time there was no water, no electricity, no heat, and no food in a city of 50,000 people, 8,000 of them children. For three days and nights there had been continuous shelling and sniper-fire within 700 metres of the city centre, and all the international personnel had left."

UNICEF negotiated with a private tourist firm for a hydrofoil that would go into Dubrovnik to negotiate a "corridor of tranquillity." Other negotiations, with Croatian and Serbian authorities, won agreement to go in to the aid of children. An Italian and a French minister, along with DeMestura were to accompany the team. They needed a fast boat to get there and one small enough not to create apprehension on the part of the besiegers. Even so, they were shelled six times on the 11-hour run down the coast and into Dubrovnik harbour, the shells landing as close as 25 metres away, although the hydrofoil was painted with a UNICEF sign and flew a UNICEF flag.

The French and Italian ministers then went to work to persuade the local military authorities to allow ships to bring in food. It was decided to use military hospital ships flying the UNICEF flag, to bring in food, medicines, and water, and bring out the wounded, the children, and pregnant and nursing mothers.

Between November 14 and December 8 there was a de facto cease-fire in Dubrovnik. A total of 6,423 children were evacuated and 3,200 tonnes of food and water brought in, according to DeMestura. By keeping the water corridor open, creating a pattern for a peaceful zone, the humanitarian assistance was delivered. On December 8 the siege of Dubrovnik was lifted.

According to Grant: "The war in Yugoslavia raised the question of whether or not the concepts contained in the Convention of the Rights of the Child apply to a war in Europe. I am glad to say that the Dubrovnik experience has demonstrated that these principles do apply." But Bouchet-Saulnier cautioned: "We must not betray the basic underlying principles of humanitarian action. Treating children differently from the rest of the civilian population, as has been done in Dubrovnik by UNICEF, may considerably weaken the very notion of 'civilian population' and the protection this population deserves."

During the latter days of the siege of Dubrovnik, when the ICRC was helping to evacuate wounded civilians, several western European countries offered their naval warships to provide escort for hospital ships, to form, as their officials put it, a "humanitarian corridor" across the Adriatic Sea to Italy. In the meantime, there were thousands of internally displaced people in the country, and the United Nations High Commissioner for Refugees expanded her mandate, as had been done in Sri Lanka, and began to look after these new-style, twentieth-century internal refugees, many of whom were eventually finding temporary refuge abroad.

By early 1992, after the United Nations had replaced the EEC in negotiating a cease-fire that worked, an estimated 10,000 people had been killed since Croatia declared independence in June 1991. The UN Security Council authorized a 14,000-man peacekeeping force to separate the combatants in three Serbian-dominated enclaves in Croatia and to oversee the disarming of the irregular forces that had caused so much havoc. This long-delayed UN operation, which was begun without the entire agreement of the parties in order to halt the killing at last, may prove to be a difficult and prolonged assignment.

Later in the spring, Bosnia-Herzegovina declared its independence, which Germany perhaps too swiftly recognized. Immediately, the same Serbian nationalism, with some Croatian complicity, began to tear this mountainous home of Muslims, Serbs, and Croats apart. The Serbian forces turned Sarajevo into a household word for ethnic infamy and "cease-fire" into a guessing game for UN peacekeepers and aid workers. UN forces were now called upon to undertake the more dangerous task of opening Sarajevo airport, as a Canadian unit under General Lewis MacKenzie did, so as to establish a fitful aerial corridor of food aid into the besieged city. UN peacekeepers were required to convoy food and medical aid shipments through this most mountainous region of Yugoslavia, harassed by Serb, Croat, and Muslim forces, to reach towns and villages cut off from food and medicine for weeks, even months, at a time. They also worked out corridors of escape for women and children wishing to leave Sarajevo or other besieged towns.

As Mary Battiata of the *Washington Post* wrote late in 1992, children who make up more than half of the 2.1 million people displaced by this civil war "have been more traumatized by the war than any other group, according to psychologists and physicians working here. That is because the children have witnessed it. Unlike the more formal battlefields of World War II, the Bosnian war, like the Croatian war that preceded it in 1991, has exploded right on children's doorsteps. It is a modern war fought in a medieval way—village against village, neighbour against neighbour, with heavy artillery trained on civilians, and their homes, churches and schools." As a result, UNICEF officials were saying that many children are showing symptoms of extreme psychological trauma, with rising numbers of child suicide, many reports of muteness, severe anxiety when separated from a parent, bed-wetting, concentration loss, sleeplessness, and deep depression.

Peacekeeping and peacemaking in the remnants of Yugoslavia threaten to sink into a greater Balkan morass unless the UN Security Council can exercise its Charter rights to resolve conflicts affecting regional peace, through negotiation backed by collective strength. But the hatred and terror created by genocidal "ethnic cleansing" and the endless shelling of non-military targets bode ill for peaceful settlement, or even for humanitarian "corridors of peace" to save the children, their families, and the elderly.

Part Four

GROWING UP PEACEFUL:
A New International Consensus

UN Charter, Article Two, paragraph seven states that:
Nothing contained in the present Charter shall authorize the United Nations to intervene in matters which are essentially within the domestic jurisdiction of any state or shall require the Members to submit such matters to settlement under the present Charter; but this principle shall not prejudice the application of enforcement measures under Chapter VII.

~ ~ ~

UN Charter, Chapter Seven, includes Articles 39 to 51 regarding: "Actions with respect to threats to the peace, breaches of the peace, and acts of aggression."

Article 41 deals with peaceful measures that may be applied to an aggressor, like economic sanctions.

Article 42 allows the Security Council, if sanctions are inadequate, to "take such action by air, sea or land forces" as may be needed to maintain or restore peace.

Article 43 asks all UN members to undertake to make available, on the call of the Security Council, armed forces and assistance to accomplish that aim.

Article 46 says plans for the use of these armed forces should be made by the Security Council with the assistance of the Military Staff Committee.

Article 47 establishes a Military Staff Committee to be responsible under the Security Council for the strategic direction of the armed forces of the UN.

~ ~ ~

UN Security Council Resolution 688, April 5, 1991. (Edited)

The Security Council,

Mindful of its duties and responsibilities under the charter of the United Nations for the maintenance of international peace and security,

Recalling Article 2, paragraph 7, of the Charter of the United Nations,

Gravely concerned by the repression of the Iraqi civilian population in many parts of Iraq, including most recently in Kurdish populated areas which led to a massive flow of refugees towards and across international frontiers and to cross border incursions, which threaten international peace and security in the region,

Reaffirming the commitment of all Member States to the sovereignty, territorial integrity and political independence of Iraq and of all States in the area,

1. Condemns the repression of the Iraqi civilian population in many parts of Iraq, including most recently in Kurdish populated areas, the consequences of which threaten international peace and security in the region;

2. Demands that Iraq, as a contribution to removing the threat to international peace and security in the region, immediately end this repression and expresses the hope in the same context that an open dialogue will take place to ensure that the human and political rights of all Iraqi citizens are respected;

3. Insists that Iraq allow immediate access by international humanitarian organizations to all those in need of assistance in all parts of Iraq and to make available all necessary facilities for their operation;

4. Requests the Secretary-General to pursue his humanitarian efforts in Iraq and to report forthwith, if appropriate on the basis of a further mission to the region, on the plight of the Iraqi civilian population, and in particular the Kurdish population, suffering from the repression in all its forms inflicted by the Iraqi authorities;

5. Requests further the Secretary-General to use all the resources at his disposal, including those of the relevent United Nations agencies, to address urgently the critical needs of the refugees and displaced Iraqi population;

6. Appeals to all Member States and to all humanitarian organizations to contribute to these humanitarian relief efforts;

7. Demands that Iraq cooperate with the Secretary-General to these ends;

8. Decides to remain seized of the matter.

THE LIMITS OF SOVEREIGNTY

The problem of sovereignty and the fear that it will be overridden by an outside power or agency has arisen in all the negotiations for successful humanitarian cease-fires. But in the cases of El Salvador, Lebanon, and the Sudan, leaders were persuaded to concede some sovereignty in the interests of medically deprived children or starving mothers and families.

We still live in a world of sovereign nation states. The United Nations organization attempts to reconcile this national sovereignty with global order. The United Nations was founded to provide, among other things, collective security against war. Collective security means member states banding together to intervene, with sanctions or a UN military force, in the activities of any sovereign nation that has breached the peace or committed acts of aggression, such as invading another country.

But the UN Charter, in dealing with this aim, did not provide a world government with the police force and judicial system needed to arrest the aggressors. It also did not anticipate the problem of two superpowers engaged in what has been known as the Cold War. Since the United States and the Soviet Union, as permanent members of the UN Security Council, had veto power over UN action, they largely thwarted any effective use of the collective security provisions in their self-proclaimed spheres of influence for decades. As well, the two superpowers, suspicious of each other, refused to establish the UN force required under Article 43 to bolster collective security. International support for such a security system disappeared somewhere between its flawed exercise in the Korean War of 1950 and its perverted usage in the Gulf War of 1990-91. The latter only happened because the Cold War was over.

One diplomat with long experience at the United Nations, Israel's Abba Eban, has said that this idea of collective security, as enunciated after the Second World War, "expressed a moral revulsion from aggression, a notion of universal human solidarity in resisting it and a concept of global cooperation on behalf of world security. These are now a part of the ideology of international relations. The notion that nation states are the sole judges of their own rights and duties has been weakened."[1] But the sacred right of sovereignty — the idea that there shall be no interference with the internal affairs of member nations of the UN, except in the case of aggression — lives on. Sovereignty thus conceived acts as a shield against imperialist designs. But unfortunately this notion has also become the last refuge for dictators, former Communist states, military leaders of Third World ex-colonies, as well as Western powers with political interests to be protected or unappetizing secrets to be hidden from the eyes of the world.

Non-intervention flourished during the Cold War, since the Soviet Union upheld the right of Communist despots to ignore human rights at home, as the United States did with Latin American dictators. Yet the UN principle of sovereignty was also, in effect, modified for the superpowers. The Soviet invasion of Hungary in 1956 and of Czechoslovakia in 1960, as well as the American intervention in Guatemala in 1954 and in the Dominican Republic in 1960, brutally interfered with the sovereignty of these nations. In the end, the West tacitly accepted the Brezhnev Doctrine, allowing the Soviet Union to intervene in Soviet satellite states, and the East was unable to halt American intervention in Nicaragua or Panama.

Harvard's foreign policy critic, Professor Stanley Hoffmann, has argued that the UN's collective security coercion, as seen during the Gulf War, is too violent and its prevention of war by diplomacy too uncertain. What about UN deterrence? He writes: "Humanitarian intervention, including by force if necessary, in order to prevent or stop [domestic repression] or massacres has often been advocated. But not only do all the difficulties entailed by the use of force arise again in such cases but the claim of sovereignty will likely be used to block efforts to intervene. Most governments and international lawyers read the UN Charter as banning the use of force for humanitarian reasons."²

If collective security is an action against a violator of the peace, peacekeeping, the UN's fall-back position when aggression has been committed, is an action to keep the fighting parties apart until some kind of truce, or peace accord, can be negotiated. And a humanitarian cease-fire is usually a temporary cessation of war for the provision of aid to civilians. It is hoped that both of these are aimed, in the long run, at conflict resolution, but both challenge the sovereignty of the nation state.

When the plan to use UN peacekeepers was introduced by Canada's Lester Pearson in 1956 to end the Suez crisis, Egypt's President Nasser invoked sovereignty. Canada's makeshift proposal — to separate the combatants and save face for the British, French, and Israeli invaders — was to Nasser's advantage. But the Egyptian president insisted that Egypt would accept the intervening presence of the United Nations Emergency Force (UNEF) only so long as Egypt had the right to dismiss it when it felt its job was done. In 1967, he kicked UNEF off Egypt's sovereign soil, precipitating the Six-Day War.

UN peacekeeping became a more widely used palliative when the UN failed to prevent a conflict. But sovereignty had to be heeded before the blue beret troops could be interposed between combatants. And the veto of any one of the five permanent members of the Security Council could prevent the keepers of the peace from going into action.

The end of the Cold War has widened the scope of UN peacekeeping operations. There are signs that national sovereignty may be in retreat. In Namibia, a UN peacekeeping operation policed the demobilization of the opposing military forces and supervised elections and the establishment of a newly independent government. UN operations supervised national elections in Nicaragua and

Haiti, and a UN peacekeeping force is embarked on a major operation to rebuild the ravaged infrastructure of Cambodia and supervise elections for a new government.

But, as many delegates to the Ottawa conference noted, Article Two, paragraph seven of the UN Charter can be an obstacle to the implementation of any humanitarian cease-fire, if the country involved insists on controlling its exclusive right to manage its internal affairs. The idea of sovereignty can hamper the call for aid to the victims of war or the international criticism of human rights abuses. At the same time, this external pressure can aggravate the tensions between foreign critic and domestic defender of sovereignty. Thus the cause of humanitarian aid or human rights may sometimes be in conflict with the cause of conflict resolution or political conciliation.

Humanitarian interventions in war zones have now raised another problem. The post-Gulf War crisis in Iraq posed a dilemma for the UN. Both the Shiite and the Kurdish people had risen up against Saddam Hussein at President Bush's instigation and were then brutally repressed or even driven out of the country by Iraqi military forces. The flood of Kurdish refugees into the mountains of Turkey and Iran presented a danger to regional security and an unwanted humanitarian burden on these neighbouring countries. The pleas of NGO aid groups and the world media coverage of mothers and children starving or dying in primitive conditions in harsh wintry weather helped galvanize action.

By a combination of unilateral U.S. military action and the passage of UN Security Council Resolution 688 on April 5, 1991, international humanitarian aid was provided inside Iraq without respect to the sovereignty of that country. Refugee camps were established under UN security guards, and food and medical aid were brought into northern Iraq for the thousands of starving victims of Iraqi repression. Nothing, however, was done for the thousands of Shiite people in the south, who either fled into the marshes or surrendered in the towns and villages.

The passage of this controversial UN resolution answered the question raised by UNICEF's James Grant at the Ottawa conference: "Could a humanitarian intervention challenge the sovereignty issue when a country grossly violates the human rights of its civilians?" According to Grant, "a whole new concept of intervention is evolving," but he warned that Resolution 688 "has set a new legal parameter that will need to be applied with great care. Smaller countries have reason to fear that the more powerful will use 688 as an excuse to move into their territory with another agenda."

Grant has also said that "many nations are apprehensive about establishing exceptions to the traditional doctrine of strict non-interference in their sovereign affairs. But the new initiative has as proponents some of the principal nations contributing to humanitarian relief in emergencies."

Here is what the Foreign Minister of Italy said to the UN General Assembly: "...the right to intervene for humanitarian ends and the protection of human rights is gaining ground. This type of intervention has become an idée-fixe, and the most truly innovative concept of the remaining decade of this century.... Intervention that is primarily aimed at securing protection of human rights and respect for the basic principles of peaceful coexistence, is a prerogative of the international community, which must have the power to suspend sovereignty whenever it is exercised in a criminal manner." The French Foreign Minister called Resolution 688 "a foundation for a new humanitarianism."

Grant echoes these sentiments and adds: "At the same time we must be aware of the concerns of nations that fear their sovereignty will be infringed." The spokesperson for the Group of 77 (developing nations) at the United Nations expressed it this way:

> Our worry stems out of our history, when many of us, as colonial subjects, had no rights. The respect for sovereignty which the UN system enjoins is not an idle stipulation which can be rejected out-

right in the name of even the most noble gestures. And an essential attribute of that sovereignty is the principle of consent, one of the cornerstones in the democratic ideal itself. And to our group it involves partners, mediations, and in our global context, a fantastic convergence of the burning desire to help, and the wonderful sense of relief in freely and willingly receiving the help. The UN cannot and must not be commandeered into forming an assistance brigade that will deliver its gifts by coercion. That will definitely be unacceptable to us.

Resolution 688 was attacked at the Ottawa conference by Eric Hoskins, the Canadian doctor who was a member of the Gulf Peace Team. "Humanitarian aid is political in its outcome," he said, "but we need to do everything in our power to ensure that the motivation for the action is not politically derived. UN Security Council Resolution 688 is an example of not respecting these principles." He charged that it was a very selective political response, not a humanitarian intervention.

Jacques de Milliano of Médecins sans Frontières pursued this further and asked: "Why is the political attention for the humanitarian situation in Somalia, Liberia, and the Sudan so low? And why was the international community, on the other hand, ready to intervene in Northern Iraq to protect the Kurdish people? And why not a humanitarian intervention in Southern Iraq in favour of the Shiite population? Yes, it has to do with politics. We should not give politicians the primary role in guarding humanitarian standards and principles. Geopolitical interests, economic considerations, and security concerns are priorities on their agendas."

This attitude to Resolution 688 was also shared by those who felt that in the Gulf War economic sanctions had not been tested, UN control of the military was absent, and the Charter was misused for political (meaning Big Power) reasons. These critics said that, in the case of post-war sanctions, food was being used as a weapon, contrary to the UN Charter. Professor John Sigler of Ottawa's Carleton University argued that Resolution 688 might be fine by itself, but it was tied to UN Resolution 678. This is the Security Council resolution that authorized the United States to lead the coalition to reverse the invasion of Kuwait, rather than acting directly under Article 42 of the Charter, which calls for a UN force to be set up to restore peace and security. Sigler told one working group that the two resolutions "will be written off as enormous errors, flawed interventions that we will learn never to use again. What were the consequences of 678, short term and long term? It is going to become increasingly clear that they were counter-productive, morally, legally, politically, and in children's terms, everything. There were alternatives."

Conversely, the North American representative of the Kurdish Front, Barham Salih, wanted the merits of Resolution 688 emphasized. Its aim should become the norm, as important as UN resolutions dismantling weapons of war, he told the working group on the Iran-Iraq corridor. The Kurdish problem had always been called an "internal affair" for Iraq, he said, and as a result of diplomatic neglect, "genocide" against the Kurds had been carried on for years before the Gulf War. Resolution 688 "overcame" some of this neglect.

In an interview, Grant said that "Resolution 688 was the first UN resolution not approved by the country involved, which has its good and bad connotations. But it does put countries on notice that it could happen to them, a United Nations intervention, if their peoples are suffering and need humanitarian help." (He may have forgotten UN resolutions intervening in South Africa and Rhodesia.) Larry Minear of the Overseas Development Council told one working group that "the Iraq option was a worst-case scenario where you have to override a government, and it is a warning to other governments that they should not put the international community in that position. In the meantime, perhaps sovereignty and humanitarian actions can be reconciled somehow. Resolution 688," he concluded, "can perhaps facilitate action involving humanitarian cease-fires."

The idea of the "right to interfere" is catching on. In September 1991, Canada's Prime Minister Brian Mulroney said in a speech at Stanford University that Canada favours "rethinking the limits of national sovereignty in a world where problems respect no borders." He went on to say that "some Security Council members have opposed intervention in Yugoslavia...on the grounds of national sovereignty. Quite frankly, such invocations of the principle of national sovereignty are as out of date and as offensive to me as the police declining to stop family violence simply because a man's home is supposed to be his castle."[3]

Brian Urquhart, former UN under-secretary-general in charge of peacekeeping affairs, wrote last year that many developments of our time are challenging the validity of the principle of national sovereignty: "Science and technology, including the incalculable effects of the communications revolution, migrations from poor to rich countries, the electronic flow of money across borders for investment and speculation, pollution and radioactive debris, the impact of new ideas or of religious movements, the traffic in drugs, AIDS, and terrorism are only a few of the phenomena that pay scant attention to national borders or sovereignty."

In the political world, loud obeisance may still be paid to the sovereignty wall around the nation state, but in the economic world, sovereignty has been eroded by the pressures of the environment and of multinational corporations, or by the pooling of sovereignty in a multi-state organization like the European Economic Community. Ahead of the Common Market countries looms change that could affect political sovereignty as well. Britain's Edward Heath, a longtime advocate of European unity, said recently that sovereignty should be exercised for the good of the people, not just the state.

The United Nations and its secretaries-general have often overcome problems created by the politics of the organization or the wording of the Charter by developing a record of precedents.

Peacekeeping itself was built upon UN precedents of intervening to obtain cease-fires in conflicts. When in 1956 the Security Council could not agree on how to deal with the Suez crisis, Pearson and UN Secretary-General Dag Hammarskjold turned to the Uniting for Peace Resolution, passed by the General Assembly in 1950. It was on the books strictly to avoid the kind of Soviet roadblock that might occur if another Korean-type invasion happened and action were vetoed in the Security Council. Taking the Suez crisis to the General Assembly allowed the first peacekeeping force to be formed, and on this basis peacekeeping has taken on the broadly based role it has today. The first UNEF created other precedents that have been built upon since. New roles for the UN in various peace activities can be built by example. But a precedent is not a precedent until it has been used as one, and who knows whether the extreme violations of human rights and egregious lack of compassion for its own citizen refugees in Iraq will be replicated elsewhere, inspiring a new Resolution 688.

Secretary-General Javier Pérez de Cuellar said in his annual report in September 1991 that "the United Nations is now entering uncharted territories and undertaking tasks of a kind unforeseen in its original design." He gave his blessing to the changed atmosphere when he said in his final report:

> It is now increasingly felt that the principle of non-interference with the essential domestic jurisdiction of States cannot be regarded as a protective barrier behind which human rights could be massively or systematically violated with impunity.... The case for not impinging on the sovereignty, territorial integrity, and political independence of States is by itself indubitably strong. But it would only be weakened if it were to carry the implication that sovereignty, even in this day and age, includes the right of mass slaughter or of launching systematic campaigns of decimation or forced exodus of populations in the name of controlling civil strife or insurrection.[4]

Urging common sense and compassion, the Secretary-General warned that "we need not impale ourselves on the horns of a dilemma between respect for sovereignty and the protection of human rights. The last thing the United Nations needs is a new ideological controversy." But in response to the insistence from everyone — from the general public to the G-7 industrial nations — that the world cannot stand idly by when thousands of children, elderly, and other non-combatants are dying in ugly civil wars, man-made famines, or actions of repressive regimes, Pérez de Cuellar articulated three caveats about interventionism. "First, like all other basic principles, the principle of protection of human rights cannot be invoked in a particular situation and disregarded in a similar one. To apply it selectively is to debase it." That should mean that if the UN can intervene for the Kurds in Iraq, it should be willing to intervene for the Somalis in Mogadishu or for the people in Yugoslavia. And if that were so, it might be thought that humanitarian cease-fires could be one way to begin the process of intervention.

"Second, any international action for protecting human rights must be based on a decision taken in accordance with the Charter of the United Nations. It must not be a unilateral act." It should not, in other words, send U.S. troops into a country before the UN Security Council has authorized UN action. Where this leaves the case of UN resolutions on Iraq is left in some ambiguity.

"Third, and relatedly, the consideration of proportionality is of the utmost importance in this respect. Should the scale or manner of international action be out of proportion to the wrong that is reported to have been committed, it is bound to evoke a vehement reaction, which, in the long run, would jeopardize the very rights that were sought to be defended." Avoid excessive force or massive intervention in dealing with dubious causes, the UN Secretary-General was saying.[5]

Cease-fires for humanitarian purposes usually involve intervention in the warlike affairs of a sovereign state. If they are designed to obtain a "corridor of peace" or "days of tranquillity," they will also involve dealing with both sides to a conflict, and each party may be exercising sovereignty over different parts of a country. Usually it means the aid intervenors must obtain the consent of both, without conferring legal recognition on the sovereignty claims of the insurgents.

In the draft communique discussed by the Ottawa conference on the final day, there was a reference to "a need to ensure the accessibility of the victims of armed conflict in all instances to humanitarian aid by reinforcing the concept that humanitarian needs take precedence over state sovereignty."[6] There was much support in the conference for the idea that suffering and human rights should outweigh the concerns of sovereignty. But this resolution was omitted in the final communique. That statement, which is the Centre for Days of Peace's articulation of the conference discussion, did say, however, that "the promise of United Nations Security Council Resolution 688 can only be realized if the principles that it establishes are not applied selectively."[7]

During the spring and summer of 1992, the question of selectivity and sovereignty were hotly debated in the UN with respect to Yugoslavia and Somalia. During the brutal Serbian war on civilians in Bosnia, UN peacekeepers secured the Sarajevo airport to provide food for the starving but were often blocked when trying to open corridors of aid to other centres in territory over which Serbian militia claimed sovereignty. The initial UN peacekeeping action to help even greater numbers of needy, starving people was ineffective in Somalia, a country where all government control had broken down and armed bands were looting food aid stations and convoys at will. The last-minute decision of the United States in late 1992 to obtain UN support for a well-armed military intervention by so-called enforcement troops to bring some order out of chaos, protect the food convoys, and disarm the roving bandits provided a new precedent for using force for humanitarian reasons. Where no sovereignty was evident, the issue was hardly raised, and cease-fires for aid were generally imposed.

UN Secretary-General Boutros Boutros-Ghali, in his important June 1992 report, "An Agenda for Peace," called for a recommitment of the UN and its Security Council to the original purposes and principles of the UN Charter, especially its preventive diplomacy and collective security provisions. He noted the "importance and indispensability of the sovereign state as a fundamental entity of the international community" and the "foundation stone of UN work." But he also reminded the members that "the time of absolute and exclusive sovereignty has passed," for "its theory was never matched by reality."[8]

THE RIGHT TO HELP

The right to humanitarian assistance is universal and enshrined in Article One of the Geneva Conventions. In other words, providing humanitarian aid can never be seen as interfering with the internal affairs of a state. This viewpoint was widely supported at the Ottawa conference and included in the final communique, which added that a humanitarian cease-fire was not considered a necessary precondition for the delivery of such aid. But, as the ICRC participant would be the first to admit, "one of the worst enemies of the Geneva Conventions is ignorance."

The Second World War revealed in horrendous detail what "total war" involved and how civilians, especially children, were the principal victims. As a result, in 1949 the Geneva Conventions, which hitherto had dealt exclusively with the rights of soldiers, were extended to the civilian population, so that they, as well as the military sick and wounded, on land and sea, and prisoners of war, would be protected. As more and more wars in this century turned out to be internal rather than international wars, and unconventional as opposed to conventional ones, two additional protocols were added in 1977. Protocol I reinforced the protection of civilians during international hostilities, including "armed conflicts against colonial domination, alien occupation, and racial regimes in the exercise of their right to self-determination."[9] Protocol II prohibited attacks against civilians, as well as terrorist threats and attacks on them in an internal war. Common to the 1949 conventions was Article Three, which along with the second protocol ensured that individuals were protected not only from acts committed by the enemy, but also those of their own government, an important step towards universal protection for victims of war.

International humanitarian law is not mandatory and, for reasons of sovereignty, is subject to the consent of a country. In *Casualties of Conflict*, Christer Ahlstrom puts it this way:

Supervision and enforcement of international law is not comparable to that of a domestic legal system. There is no international police force or court with a mandate to supervise the law's implementation and enforcement. It is up to states themselves to show the international community that they are trustworthy by meeting the obligations which they have undertaken in good faith.

One alternative view which has gained some support in recent years, however, is that states party to the Geneva Conventions have a collective obligation to see that these treaties are universally respected. According to Article 1 which is common to all Geneva Conventions, states have undertaken **"to respect and ensure respect for the Convention in all circumstances."**[10]
(Author's emphasis)

In this era of change and the recognition and promotion of the rights of children and civilians in general, there have been encouraging developments, beginning of course with the UN Convention on the Rights of the Child, which came into force on September 2, 1990. It defines a child as "every human being below the age of 18 years unless, under the law applicable to the child, majority is attained earlier." It calls on states to "recognize the right of the child to the enjoyment of the highest attainable standard of health and to facilities for the treatment of illness and rehabilitation of health."[11] It also deals with children in war and in situations where torture and inhuman punishment is inflicted, a common feature of civil wars.

Article 38 of this convention outlines the obligations of states "to respect and to ensure respect for rules of international humanitarian law applicable to them in armed conflicts which are relevant to the child." It also makes an effort to wipe out the increasingly prevalent category of "child soldier." It urges that the recruitment and participation of children under 15 years in armed conflict should be stopped. When the draft convention was being debated, only one country opposed the general consensus that the age should be raised to at least 17 or 18 years. That country was the United States, which to date has neither signed nor ratified the Convention on the Rights of the Child. Article 39, in dealing with armed conflict, calls on states to take appropriate measures to promote physical and psychological recovery and social reintegration of child victims. Article 37, among other things, prohibits the torture of children, the imposition of the death penalty, and the arbitrary deprivation of their liberty, too frequently the fate for youngsters in civil war zones or under repressive regimes.

While these articles bind states, they do not bind insurgent or guerrilla groups, who are often the most frequent users, and misusers, of child soldiers. A recent report by British Quakers shows Afghan children of 9 fighting in the jihad, Cambodian children of 12 abducted for service by the Khmer Rouge, Guatemalan children of 8 out on civil defence patrols, and Sri Lankans of 10 years of age forced to enrol in the armed militia. The Quakers, and several countries who signed the convention, have proposed that an additional protocol be added to the convention to state that recruitment into the armed forces should not be allowed for people under 18 years. The Quakers also add that younger children fleeing such recruitment should be declared to be refugees entitled to international protection.

Already, however, according to Defence for Children International in its 1992 brief to the International Commission on Human Rights in Geneva, there are a number of countries that have "reservations" to the convention.[12] Burma (Myanmar), which is engaged in a brutal civil war, deposited a reservation to Article 37 on torture and death for juveniles. Kuwait's reservation was against "all provisions of the convention that are incompatible with the laws of Islamic *sharia* and the local statutes." Somewhat similar reservations have been made by Pakistan, Bangladesh, Egypt, Jordan, Iran, Afghanistan, Mauritania, and the Maldives.

As Defence for Children International said, while 109 countries had ratified the convention, the growing number of "reservations" could threaten to render the rights of the child meaningless in regions where it is most necessary. This is another case where states need to learn to abide by international humanitarian law and educate their people to observe these rights in full. As James Grant said, "we must insist that governments and other combatants implement all the articles" protecting children.

To many of the participants at the Ottawa conference, this meant targeting the military forces. Educating the soldiers in a regular army should be a priority of governments, but it should also apply to insurgent forces, as was pointed out in the case of the Sudan. The importance of reaching and persuading guerrilla forces like those in Somalia or Mozambique or Sri Lanka was stressed in the working groups, and the difficulty of doing so was recognized. The idea that training films for combatants might be made available as part of peace education was suggested, but if there are leaders or officers on either side who will not use them, little may be accomplished. At the same time, it was urged by many participants that humanitarian aid NGOs should know their rights under the Geneva Conventions, and that violations of international humanitarian law should be publicized by aid groups and the international media. Donor countries, international aid agencies, and NGOs must also recognize their responsibilities under these global codes of conduct. Education on rights and peace education were widely urged during this conference.

Lieutenant Colonel Christian Harleman, director of the UN Institute for Training and Research (UNITAR), suggested in one working group that UN peacekeeping was more adaptable today than ever before and might therefore be of assistance in implementing humanitarian cease-fires or "days of tranquillity." He said there was more of a role for regional peacekeeping and that it might be possible to establish regional UN training centres where both government and insurgent forces could be trained in the humanitarian conduct of war and in the Geneva Conventions. The concept of peace education could also be encouraged in such a centre, and it might be instrumental in changing views on both sides.

The Organization of African Unity (OAU) has tried for years to mediate African conflicts based on borders set in colonial days, by observing the "integrity" of those borders. Today, the OAU is seeking a new role. In 1990 the organization made a decision in favour of the rights of citizens. It passed a resolution supporting the concept of special measures to be extended to civilians in conflict zones and endorsed the idea of "children as a zone of peace" with rights to be protected.

The 1990 World Summit for Children passed a Plan of Action to implement the world declaration on the survival, protection, and development of children. The Plan of Action's Article 25 encourages the use of humanitarian cease-fires and "corridors of peace" to help children in war. The Ottawa conference represented an attempt to broaden this concept, to widen understanding of the rights of children, to understand regions where "zones of peace" might be helpful, and to discuss new ideas about how to protect children, and other civilians, in some "new world order."

While this conference was meeting, an interesting debate was going on at the United Nations. For some time there had been criticism of the way UN relief agencies stumbled over each other in natural disasters, like that in Bangladesh in 1991, or in areas of conflict like the Horn of Africa. In late December, the UN General Assembly passed a resolution, drafted by Sweden with the support of other Nordic countries, Canada, the United States, and the European Economic Community, to establish a new system for co-ordinating UN humanitarian assistance. So that disaster agencies wouldn't be tripping over themselves any more, a new high-level emergency relief co-ordinator would be appointed, designated by the UN secretary-general and with direct access to him. He would have an emergency fund of $50 million (U.S.) at his disposal and more flexible powers to act.

The resolution states that "humanitarian assistance must be provided in accordance with the principles of humanity, neutrality and impartiality." But, paying minimum tribute to sovereignty, it said that this assistance should be provided with the consent of the affected country, and "in principle" on the basis of an appeal by that country. The UN relief co-ordinator can thus initiate negotiations, without a request from a reluctant government, so as to permit an urgent relief effort to be started. The UN, presumably, is not going to take an initial "no" for an answer in a desperate situation.

One Canadian news report quoted UN sources in explanation: "This new flexibility will allow the UN to provide relief (or actively push for it) in countries where there is no governmental authority, such as Somalia; in a country where a government would refuse aid because it is actively repressing its population, such as Iraq; or in a country that has a policy of national self-sufficiency that makes it reluctant to petition for aid, such as the Philippines."[13]

As far as aid to children in war zones is concerned, the emergency relief co-ordinator has among his many responsibilities "actively facilitating, including through negotiation if needed, the access by the operational organizations to emergency areas for the rapid provision of emergency assistance by obtaining the consent of all parties concerned, through modalities such as the establishment of temporary relief corridors where needed, days and zones of tranquillity and other forms."[14] Cutting away the turgid verbiage of the UN bureaucrats, it means the co-ordinator can, if it is useful, seek to obtain "days of peace" or "corridors of aid" in conflict zones through cease-fires or other means, so that medical aid and food can be delivered to children and other civilians.

Larry Minear, now working with the Refugee Policy Group as co-director of a project on "Humanitarianism and War," said: "The co-ordination task, which has political as well as humanitarian dimensions, can make a difference for people in need of assistance throughout the world." He said NGOs would welcome the appointment in March 1992 of Jan Eliasson, Sweden's permanent UN representative, as emergency relief co-ordinator with rank of under-secretary-general. "The new co-ordinator faces complex challenges," he said in a written statement. "Late last year the General Assembly, in part through Eliasson's own efforts, encouraged a more assertive approach to reaching people in need. It recommended specific strategies which have proven effective in recent years, such as temporary relief corridors and days and zones of tranquillity. Assuring and capitalizing on access to people in situations of civil conflict requires working in the vortex of political and humanitarian cross-currents and helping disparate institutions work together. The task will not be easy. However, all who are committed to a more effective international system of assistance and protection wish him well." He added that major humanitarian crises in Somalia and Iraq will be an early test of his skills.

Minear and others at the Ottawa conference also urged the United Nations to take action to provide some UN aid agencies with greater rights in dealing with conflict situations, such as UNICEF already has. UN operating agencies, like the World Food Programme and the UN High Commissioner for Refugees, should have the right and responsibility to work with all parties to a conflict in order to enable the delivery of humanitarian assistance in a transparent fashion, without this being perceived as a threat or breach of national sovereignty, or as bestowing recognition on rebel insurgents. It was the inability of the UN agencies to move in Somalia, paralysed by present UN constraints regarding sovereignty, that spawned some of these proposals.

Colonel Harleman of UNITAR said in another interview that his organization has been "developing UNHAT, UN Humanitarian Assistance Teams." This idea would make unarmed teams available to help the new relief coordinator in his tasks of providing aid, especially in areas of conflict or disasters resulting from war. Whether UNHAT teams become part of the UN aid agenda depends on how the new humanitarian relief co-ordination system actually works out.

Among the responsibilities of the new emergency relief co-ordinator is one to provide consolidated information on disaster situations, "including early warning on emergencies." This important concern was raised at the Ottawa conference by Abdul Mohammed, director of the Inter-Africa Group. He urged that "there must be some mechanism that will trigger UN action in these emergency situations." It could be the Stockholm International Peace Institute's guideline which designates as a war any conflict that leaves 1,000 dead, or a designation based on the number of refugees forced to flee, or the lack of a coherent government, all indicators of a disaster in the making and the need for world action. The Ottawa conference in its final communique called for an impartial body with "the responsibility to identify and evaluate situations of conflict, and to inform the international community where international intervention for the purposes of humanitarian assistance may be warranted."[15] It will be interesting to see if the UN emergency relief co-ordinator's early warning function develops in this fashion.

Robin Hay pointed out in his background paper on the "Civilian Aspects of United Nations Peacekeeping" that a number of experts, like Indar Jit Rikhye, Thomas Weiss, and Aage Eknes, have speculated on the use of military peacekeeping troops in securing the right to deliver humanitarian aid. None of the UN relief agencies has a built-in security component, although, as the conference heard, the Red Cross (ICRC) has had armed guards on its trucks in the Horn of Africa for the first time in its history. Weiss is quoted as saying that peacekeeping troops could prove useful in the "contemporary world as part of a more comprehensive international response to humanitarian crises." The catch in this, as the troop-led humanitarian exercise to save the Kurds in Iraq revealed, is that aid agencies following in the wake of the military or arriving in army helicopters find their credibility undercut by their new associations.

Brian Urquhart, the former UN under-secretary-general in charge of peacekeeping, goes beyond this in calling for a new category of UN operation, "somewhere between peacekeeping and large-scale enforcement. It would be intended to put an end to random violence (as in Somalia or Yugoslavia) and to provide a reasonable degree of peace and order so that the rights to humanitarian relief could be observed, the aid work could go forward and a conciliation process could commence. The forces involved would be relatively small, representatively international, and would not have military objectives as such. But unlike peacekeeping forces, such troops would be required to take, initially at least, certain combat risks in bringing the violence under control They would essentially be armed police actions."[16] But they would be carried out in defence of people's rights to humanitarian assistance. And he says again the old ideas about "the sacrosanct nature of domestic jurisdiction" must change.

The first report from UN Secretary-General Boutros Boutros-Ghali in June 1992, *An Agenda for Peace*, spelled out some of these proposals in his call for implementing UN articles 43 and 47 on collective security. He also suggested early warning measures that would include preventive deployment of a UN presence before a conflict starts, either in an internal or external crisis where humanitarian aid is involved, and he even proposed that demilitarized zones be established, with agreement of both sides, before war materializes, to encourage political negotiation and to secure the rights to aid for any refugees of the crisis.

This "militarized" approach might pose serious problems for humanitarian work, as NGO aid workers pointed out. But this was before the United States and other nations intervened with armed force in Somalia to help save millions from death. As Nancy Gordon, communications director of CARE Canada, wrote in supporting this harsh prescription: "Echoes of colonial times haunt the international community, particularly those involved in development and relief. But there are standards of decency, standards that embody respect for human life, for dignity, standards that many states have adopted through the various covenants on human rights. These have become international standards and we must not allow them to be ignored or tainted by claims of sovereignty and non-interference in the internal affairs of states."[17] Might in the cause of humanity could, in certain circumstances, be right.

CORRIDORS OF TRANQUILLITY

Historically, silencing the guns of war for humanitarian reasons has served the practical purpose of removing the wounded and dead from the battlefield. But today's humanitarian cease-fire, as we have seen, serves a new and different objective, which calls for a fresh look at its definition.

"Days of peace" and "corridors of tranquillity" have already brought necessary health care and food relief to hundreds of thousands of children and families in the war zones of the world. But there were those at the Ottawa conference who objected to this terminology. As Jacques de Milliano of Médecins sans Frontières pointed out, "the problem with humanitarian cease-fires is that they are part of the logic of war for military thinkers." Others, like Larry Minear, agreed, saying that "the concept of humanitarian cease-fires is in some ways too narrow to address the issues we are talking about."

Abdul Mohammed of the Inter-Africa Group suggested that "perhaps it should be called 'humanitarian accessibility.'" The idea is to obtain access to children, caregivers, and the elderly in impossible situations, thus bringing them hope and aid. That access could be through corridors on land, sea, or in the air, or by "days of peace" or "tranquillity."

The Ottawa conference tried to summarize the basic features of humanitarian cease-fires after reviewing the successful ones and listening to the critiques brought by other observers.

- Often such cease-fires are brought about by the pressure of the international community, as in El Salvador or the Sudan. Yet, to be successful, they need to exhibit transparency and impartiality in their operation, so that neither side to a conflict needs fear being put at a disadvantage.

- It is essential to develop trust between people prior to agreeing to a cease-fire, and this requires considerable communication.

- International agencies with the clout to bring about a cease-fire, as well as NGOs that may carry out the work in the "days of peace," must know what the roots of the conflict are. They must also be known in the region by the parties to the dispute.

- NGOs on the scene, as one participant said, "must be humanitarian by impetus, but political in their understanding." While remaining neutral, they must be aware of the political problems their aid activity brings so that the operation is not bungled through ignorance or naivete. That can be accomplished by ensuring that indigenous national and local NGOs and grass-roots organizations are included in the humanitarian process.

- It is possible that the two parties in a conflict might never actually sit down at the same table together. They may dialogue through a third party acceptable to both sides.

- There is an initial need to overcome government suspicion that a humanitarian cease-fire may be used by the opposition to rebuild its forces and defences. The same applies in reverse with the forces of the insurgency. This general concern is why the use of the term "cease-fire" must often be replaced with "days" or "zones of tranquillity."

- The negotiating dialogue must spell out clearly the principles of the operation and what is to be allowed through as aid: medicines, vaccines, food, and so forth.

- There has to be an exact delimitation of the "zones of tranquillity" or the "corridors of aid," clear identification of the trucks, trains, or boats to be used, and an assurance that no arms will be transported or military information passed.

- Time limits have to be defined. A short period may turn out to be too short for, say, proper immunization of the children or for delivery of aid to remote areas. A long period may create what aid experts call the "relief dependency syndrome" and ensure that real peace talks never get started. Or if the period is too long, the chances for the cease-fire to break down may increase. Both periods of time may encourage false hopes of peace that then discourage conflict resolution.

- Since the United Nations must often play a role in these cease-fire situations, as Larry Minear has said, "mobilizing world opinion, generating resources, demonstrating international presence, and ensuring liaison with governmental authorities," the division of labour between the UN, the NGOs, and the governments in obtaining the cease-fire and establishing the "corridors" or "days of peace" is important and should be based on the different capacities of the various organizations involved.

Minear also warned that "the structural bias of the UN towards governments suggests that the system itself is not yet properly structured to respond to crises in which insurgents constitute a de facto authority in a position to challenge the authority of an internally recognized government."[18] That was why the World Food Programme and the UN Development should have the same powers that UNICEF has to deal with insurgents in organizing these humanitarian interventions.

Chris Giannou, the Canadian doctor who has worked in Lebanon and Cambodia, warned the conference that "humanitarian work is political, don't fool yourselves." Often, of course, it is political pressure resulting from public concern over a civil war or refugee disaster that encourages the call for cease-fires. Then it is often obvious that there are political, not humanitarian, reasons on both sides of a conflict that support such cease-fires. As Bouchet-Saulnier of Médecins sans Frontières said, "A cease-fire always implies negotiations with military authorities and the making of certain compromises.... A cease-fire remains part and parcel of hostilities. We would be deceiving ourselves if we believed that a truce was not being used for military purposes." At the same time, some participants in the conference noted that the United Nations itself was political in its actions: it could move to help Sudan, but not Somalia; it could be involved today in Cambodia, but not in Liberia or the West Bank of Israel. Chris Giannou even argued that earlier UN political decisions to allow the war against the Vietnamese-installed Cambodian government to continue meant humanitarian aid to the Cambodian refugees abroad helped prolong the conflict.

Some people noticed that the presence of international aid organizations sometimes tended to inhibit the excessively ruthless activities of the military in war zones. But other participants pointed out that the presence of UN agencies was not always welcomed in places like Ethiopia or Sri Lanka, because local insurgents did not trust such foreign intervention. The differences for NGOs and international agencies between working in government-held areas and in rebel-held areas was discussed and compared with working in "grey areas," where neither side controls the territory and the danger is roving bandits or freelance militiamen, as in the Sudan. There was also the problem of communication between rebel commanders in a widely dispersed war, as in Mozambique, and their failure to accept a cease-fire. Cease-fire aid convoys might be highly vulnerable to attack. But those who had been involved, like Solomon Gidada of Ethiopia, said humanitarian aid workers assume these risks for the sake of the children and families.

UNICEF's Egyptian representative, Baquer Namazi, concluded that "the conceptual framework of humanitarian cease-fires or 'zones of peace' for children must be constructed for each region to take account of the nature and special conditions of conflict and the peace potential in each area. Through unrelenting advocacy by NGOs, religious leaders, and professional groups who are committed to humanitarianism, the regional and political decision makers must be sensitized to the ideas and their usage." But Bouchet-Saulnier cautioned that "the use of new humanitarian concepts in recent years—the right to intervene, survival corridors, and humanitarian corridors—along with the challenge of providing humanitarian help—must not conceal the terrible weakness of these notions in the face of grave and brutal violations of conventional humanitarian law," as seen in Yugoslavia.

Giannou, who worked recently in Somalia, looked at the conditions necessary for a cease-fire to operate. He said that in Somalia, where rival forces may be of the same clan, prospects of a success were possible. But that in the West Bank and the Gaza Strip the possibilities were dim, unless the Middle East peace talks were successful. As for Iraq, with its highly politicized situation and the UN intervention, there might be no need for such a cease-fire. Aid could be put in place by enforcing humanitarian rules of conduct.

However, there were also seemingly intractable situations: as in Burma (Myanmar), where a government deliberately tries to cut the country and its civil war off from all outside influences; in the Bosnian civil war, where there are three parties to the dispute; or in Somalia, where the country is in chaos and no government exists. Then these precepts for humanitarian intervention may be thrown out the window. Perhaps only the pressure of global opprobrium or the collective political will exerted on the problem by the United Nations can make a difference. But it was agreed that the scope for testing the use of such "humanitarian accessibility" through cease-fires was wide-ranging and, given the proclivity of man for conflict, most urgently worth pursuing.

BUILDING BLOCKS FOR PEACE

"We have been moving borders, important borders, the borders in our minds," as Jacques de Milliano of Médecins sans Frontières put it so felicitously when the Ottawa conference was nearing its conclusion.

This conference was inspired by compassion for children in the tragic situation of wars not of their making. It was built on the hope that humanitarian cease-fires might produce "days," "zones," or "corridors of peace" that might help to provide children with medicines, food, or other assistance necessary for their survival. It was based on the desire to expand the core values of humanity, in a global fashion, on behalf of those who are the future of our world.

The conference heard about the unspeakable horrors faced by children in Mozambique, the unending warfare in Somalia, the effects of starvation in the Sudan and Ethiopia, the tragic victims of the Gulf War in Iraq, the torment of civil wars in Sri Lanka, Burma (Myanmar), the Philippines, and Colombia, the grim struggles in Lebanon and El Salvador, and the unending civilian slaughter in Yugoslavia. But the participants who brought these tales of death and destruction found the exchange of views and experiences helpful and enlightening. Minds indeed may have been changed, perhaps in unexpected ways. Certainly the sponsors of this conference learned that children are not the only ones who need help in war. All civilians do. They learned that in some countries children do not come first in times of war. They learned that humanitarian cease-fires are not applicable in many conflict situations, and that even the name is thought by some to have too militaristic a connotation. Each conflict situation calls for a different approach. They learned that building on "days of tranquillity" does not always lead to conflict resolution or peacebuilding. But more importantly, more positively, they learned that the whole concept is extremely valuable and worth propagating in a world where war and civil violence is still, unfortunately, far too prevalent. Perhaps like peacekeeping, which was not initially well understood, it will gain credibility over time.

The spirit that humanitarian assistance brings to war situations was first seen in conflicts earlier than those of El Salvador. In Nigeria, during the height of the 1968 Biafran civil war, UNICEF's executive director Henry Labouisse quietly persuaded Nigeria's leader, General Yakubu Gowon, that the agency's concern for children and other civilians on both sides of the conflict did not imply support for the Biafran secessionists. As a result, two months later, Nigeria allowed separate airlifts, organized by the ICRC and church agencies and using UNICEF food and medical supplies, to enter the blockaded Biafra region. NGOs in such situations may have even more freedom than UN organizations, as the Quakers found. Dealing with both the Biafrans and the Nigerian government, they played a conciliatory role that may have had a moderating effect on how the Nigerians dealt with their Biafran brothers when they won the war, according to Mike Yarrow's book, *Quaker Experiences in International Conciliation*. Peaceful reconciliation after this fratricidal war, was the watchword in Nigeria, to the surprise of many outside observers. This early example of using "humanitarian accessibility" to help in the peacebuilding process is not always possible, but it shows how aid-givers can become a conciliating force in a conflict situation. As neutral and respected sources available to both sides, they have an opportunity to encourage understanding and promote ideas that may help to solve some of the basic problems that caused the war.

Naturally, there were some sceptics at the Ottawa conference. A cautionary assessment of the cease-fire/peacebuilding idea was provided early on by Pierre Gassman, who gained his experience in humanitarian operations in Africa. He said that we tend to assume humanitarian cease-fires are a positive goal, then we progress from this assumption to peacebuilding. But humanitarian cease-fires are imperfect things, useful only if applied to emergency situations. And we should be wary of our motives: the idea of saving children for a day may simply be gratifying Western sensibilities. We also gratify ourselves by projecting our own priorities, like the Pope calling for a cease-fire at Christmas or Easter, which is akin to the exoneration and gratification of confession. This focus on children is a Western concept frequently not shared by other cultures. For example, in Biafra, the priorities were not the children, women, or elderly; they had a war to fight. Gassman went on to argue that one may create false hopes by advertising "days of peace." Only a few medical personnel can help a few children in a particular place at a particular time. Chance decides who is helped. Parents whose children are left out are frustrated.

Gassman insisted that "a humanitarian commitment can only facilitate the peace process, it cannot replace negotiations and dialogue on a political, military, and economic level." However, he added that "if we leave the humanitarian questions unanswered, given the global atmosphere of ever-increasing violence, these conflicts will be exacerbated." In bringing people together on these questions, he said, "a humanitarian cease-fire can be the foundation on which further dialogue can be built." But he believed that both sides to a conflict needed to abide by such rules as the Geneva Conventions and the Rights of Children, "the most complete humanitarian tools we have, to date," inadequate though they may be. They could create that degree of humanity necessary to continue the dialogue on a political level for peace. "If humanitarian cease-fires could achieve that kind of dialogue, it would be no mean achievement."

Chris Giannou, who felt humanitarian cease-fires had not solved the problems in Lebanon, said we should not let these cease-fires "be a simple pretext for reinforcing the status quo of an unjust and violent system." Peace alone, he argued, may not be the most important thing, but the causes of war are.

Recognizing the difficulties and the novelty of the concept of the humanitarian cease-fire, what has it to offer in the larger context of peacemaking, of bringing such wars to an end?

The short answer was given by Bouchet-Saulnier of Médecins sans Frontières: "Cease-fire operations make a very modest contribution to the return of peace." The more enthusiastic James Grant of UNICEF said: "My answer is yes, but more often than not they contribute indirectly. We should not count on peacebuilding happening. When we can initiate an intervention on behalf of civilians, this is an end in itself. If you can help create a space where negotiations towards peace happen, then that is a bonus, but it should not be considered as a prime goal."

However, Edmundo Garcia, who had reported on the grassroots efforts of Filipinos to obtain "zones of life" in their war regions, felt that humanitarian cease-fires could have a lasting impact inside the framework of the peace process: "Humanitarian action has a maximum impact if it is not totally divorced from the peace process." That was another argument for expanding the effort to push "education for peace," he said.

Dr. Mark Schneider of the Pan American Health Organization, who worked on the El Salvadoran cease-fires and the Central American immunization "Bridge for Peace" campaign that followed, said: "The very act of negotiating a humanitarian cease-fire can open the door for further political negotiations. One must remember that the ultimate objective is the humanitarian objective. The process of negotiating a humanitarian cease-fire can create a dynamic that allows the parties to directly confront the issues, depending on the context of the war and the parties involved in the conflict." But he had to admit that sometimes this aid can also prolong and exacerbate a conflict.

Chris Giannou argued: "You cannot judge the success or failure of a humanitarian aid operation by how much it contributed to a peace process. But if humanitarian aid can provide space to open a political dialogue it is an added benefit. It should not be the objective of a humanitarian initiative." Besides, he said at another point, "peacebuilding initiatives in one society are not necessarily applicable to another society." But if the key were found to unlock the peacemaking initiative, that effort should be closely linked to peacebuilding, the reconstruction and reformation that would eliminate the causes of the war in the first place.

In winding up the panel discussions, de Milliano spoke of the conference trying to find "an integration point" between humanitarian assistance as an act of humanity and cease-fires as a political-military act. Humanitarian organizations want to keep their principles of universality, neutrality, and impartiality intact, especially in the field. "On the other hand, humanizing conflict is not enough. We want to build peace."

He spoke of the time 20 years ago when MSF was formed. "We began our work using cross-border operations and defending the right of civilians to receive humanitarian assistance regardless of where they lived. We did not accept that the sovereignty of borders took precedence over the rights of people to basic needs. In the beginning our stance was considered too political. Now this kind of humanitarian operation is standard. It is seen as a humanitarian act, not a political act. This is an example of finding the integration point between humanitarian impetus and political motivation."

Robin Hay, in his study of cease-fires and peacebuilding wrote: "Humanitarian cease-fires indicate that the parties to a conflict are capable of cooperating to realize a superordinate goal. Moreover it demonstrates that they are able and willing to stop fighting to achieve that goal.... In this sense the humanitarian cease-fire can be used as an occasion to advocate understanding between the parties that through peace not through fighting they can solve their problems."[19]

Humanitarian co-operation of this sort can change the perceptions that parties to a conflict have about each other and can foster a trust between two sides that might help the process of negotiating peace. Given the new importance that the United Nations has recently given to emergency humanitarian aid and "days of tranquillity," this may provide another "superordinate goal" for testing the peacebuilding possibilities of humanitarian cease-fires.

And the idea is getting around. One study by Alexander Thier at Brown University considered the El Salvador case as an example of a humanitarian confidence-building measure to end war, noting that such measures address the causes of conflict: human suffering, inequity, and mistrust. Such a confidence-building measure provides a "common ground, a basic necessity of conflict resolution processes, the establishment of which humanizes the conflict by addressing a concern (e.g. children) to which all sides can relate."[20]

A recent book about Third World conflict and development, *Aid as Peacemaker*, discusses immunization cease-fires, which "present an opportunity for meeting a defined world goal of universal immunization, while they also have a very small but potentially important impact on the ability of belligerents to move toward a peaceful settlement of their dispute." Robert Miller, the editor of the book, writes about the new linkage between peacebuilding and humanitarian aid, and observes that "if famine is at least partially responsible for war, then famine relief must be concerned to end war." Non-governmental aid or "interventions that are quantitatively small, if they are seen as morally right and based on an accurate assessment of the situation, have a significant impact on peace and conflict resolution."[21]

This brief study of new innovations in "humanitarian accessibility" and assistance for children and others has shown that while old viewpoints are crumbling, older antagonisms and newer conflicts are springing up everywhere to test the new humanitarian visions. As we look at the plight of children, the elderly, and other civilians in the killing streets of Mogadishu, in the repressive militarized atmosphere of poverty-stricken Haiti, or in Liberia, whose brutal butchery was forgotten in the wake of the Gulf War, the world's humanitarian institutions often appear to be overwhelmed by an ocean of misery.

The conference could come to no definitive conclusions about humanitarian cease-fires, because the world's conflict situations are so varied, the history, culture, and traditions of the combatants so mixed, and the ability to use them so dependent on timing, patience, political will, and usually, unfortunately, the weight of the suffering. But it was agreed that such cease-fires are tremendously useful and might contribute to peacebuilding. Probably most people today would agree that sovereign nations should recognize, not oppose, the humanitarian imperatives in times of civil war and extreme emergencies and allow intervention across borders.

Conference participants agreed on "the need to ensure humanitarian aid is available to victims of armed conflict in all instances, by reinforcing the concept that humanitarian aid takes highest priority." There was agreement that other forms of violence affecting children, such as the effect of sanctions against Iraq or territorial occupation in the West Bank of Israel, demand equally imaginative proposals to permit children in such conflict areas to be reached. Finally, there was widespread agreement that peace education in many situations may be a necessity before humanitarian cease-fires can be implemented — education for the children's future and education to encourage the observation of humanitarian codes of conduct by the combatants. Unmentioned in the final communique but often alluded to in conference workshops was the useful role the media can play in covering humanitarian catastrophes and "days of peace" operations, awakening the world to tragedy and serving as a kind of public conscience that helps people recognize both need and possibilities.

Anna Mansour, a UNICEF officer in Lebanon in charge of its peace education camps, provided a definition of the peace most would want to build. "Peace goes beyond cease-fire agreements among fighters. It builds on social justice, dignity, and democracy.

It is anchored in security felt in the body and the mind. It is based on self-confidence and trust in each other. It is confirming acceptance and respect for differences, whether sectarian, regional, social, or political. It stems from respect for each other and the world in which we live, particularly the environment. It is believing in solidarity, fraternity, co-operation, and international understanding."

This conference, the participants agreed, should be the beginning of an ongoing process, so that its concepts can be reviewed and amplified in further meetings or in other forums, and the ideas spread as widely as possible. There is presently a paucity of information in this field.

"Children as a zone of peace" should not be dismissed as either utopian or naive, but seen as an inspirational call for change and humanitarian invention against the follies of the adult world. At a time when there is some slow, painful movement at the United Nations towards a broader allegiance than the nation-state, at least on humanitarian issues, it behooves people concerned about the suffering of children and other civilian victims of war to speak out, to propose and investigate new concepts, to shake up the status quo. It will not be easy or uncontroversial, but as the conference's chief rapporteur, Dr. Nola Seymoar, a Canadian public policy adviser and psychotherapist, summed it up: "We are flying in uncharted territory and need to share our maps."

Part Five

PEACEBUILDING FOR CHILDREN:
A Manifesto

Preamble

In the mid-1980s, Nils Thedin, head of Sweden's delegation to the UNICEF Executive Board, began speaking of "children as a zone of peace." The underlying intention of this concept has inspired many actions — among them, "days of tranquillity" to vaccinate and provide other humanitarian services for children and their families in zones of armed conflict.

Over the past four days we have participated in a unique meeting. For the first time people who have been involved in humanitarian cease-fires in different countries, representatives of international agencies, non-governmental organizations, governments, and academic institutions have come together with people from areas involved in armed conflicts to share experiences and insights, assess the lessons of past cases, and identify the potential of humanitarian cease-fires for future longer term peacebuilding. The conference has involved approximately one hundred participants, a third of whom come from 12 conflict zones. Because it is the first international conference on this topic, it is the beginning of a learning process. Thus we do not presume to do more than identify some of the issues for consideration and present a few proposals for action.

Throughout our discussions we have been reminded of the many millions who are innocent victims of war; and the millions of children and families who experience daily violence because military and economic power come before human and ecological well being. More wars have been fought in the last 10 years than in any other decade in history. The very nature of war has changed substantially. Civilian casualties have grown from 10 per cent in the First World War to 75 per cent in the 39 wars which raged in the 1980s.

While the situation of children in armed conflicts has deteriorated over the past four decades, international mechanisms for coping with their problems have improved substantially. Humanitarian agencies are increasingly well organized to provide emergency relief on a massive scale and the legal basis for the protection of children which exists in the Geneva Conventions has been elaborated in the Convention of the Rights of the Child, which was adopted unanimously by the 46th UN General Assembly in September 1989, and the "World Declaration" and "Plan of Action" of the World Summit for Children adopted in September 1990. These agreements have established a new context in which coordinated action may be taken to ease the desperate plight of millions of children who suffer the traumatic consequences of international and intranational conflicts.

At this meeting we have focused our attention on humanitarian cease-fires. In recent years, "corridors of peace" or "days of tranquillity" have been implemented with varying degrees of success in several conflict zones; with these words being substituted for "cease-fire" which carries with it certain legal connotations. We examined in some detail the cases of the Sudan, El Salvador, Lebanon, and Iraq.

In addition, we have learned of community-based initiatives called "zones of peace" in Colombia and the Philippines, which have developed without the involvement of UN agencies, and which involve communities in building a peace plan for resolving conflicts without resorting to arms. In the Philippines these communities are linked in networks and are part of a National Peace Conference.

Days/zones of tranquillity and corridors of peace have already brought needed food relief and health care to hundreds of thousands of children in areas of conflict. At this meeting there has been general agreement that these proven humanitarian methods should be extended/adopted/adapted both for their own sake and as potential peacebuilding strategies wherever possible. These initiatives are not appropriate for every war zone, nor at any or all times. They are simply a step on the road to dispute resolution. We should not expect a humanitarian cease-fire itself to resolve a conflict.

We have learned that days/zones of tranquillity and corridors of peace serve not only to expedite immediate humanitarian relief efforts on behalf of women and children, but may also transform the conditions of warfare by providing a channel for cooperation between combatants, thereby moving conflicting parties closer to negotiated settlement.

The following issues have been discussed and are offered for further analysis by participants and others interested in this process. We can only provide a partial picture of the dialogue and debate in which we have actively participated for four days. We recognize the complexity of the issues and the difficulty of conveying the context of each statement. More important we find ourselves unable adequately to express the human feelings we have experienced, to share our tears and laughter, our frustration and joy, or to communicate to others the respect and caring which has been demonstrated by and between participants regardless of which region, country, or party they represent. We feel a strong need to continue our own process of reflection and learning and recommend both further meetings and the establishment of an informal newsletter to keep one another abreast of initiatives in this new field. We are flying in uncharted territory and need to share our maps.

Themes Discussed

I. Definitions and Principles

1. There is a need to ensure that humanitarian aid is available to victims of armed conflict in all instances by reinforcing the concept that humanitarian aid takes highest priority.
2. All human interventions must be founded on a deep understanding and respect for indigenous cultures.

3. Humanitarian cease-fires may fulfill two functions: they meet human needs through the delivery of adequate supplies of required aid; and they can be part of a larger process of peacebuilding. When it is appropriate, the opportunities that present themselves for conflict resolution should be capitalized upon. The early examples of days/zones of tranquillity make clear that the process improves the potential for peacemaking dialogues. Whether it is deliberately used may be situation specific.
4. The conceptual and definitional problem of humanitarian cease-fires is an issue that needs further consideration. Distinctions between peacemaking, peacekeeping, and peacebuilding should be clarified.
5. Greater attention needs to be paid to the other types and situations of violence of which children are victims, including current economic sanctions and territorial occupations taking place for example in the Middle East. If these forms of violence are to be alleviated, measures as imaginative as humanitarian cease-fires need to be developed. Humanitarian cease-fires are not necessarily applicable in these different contexts. In various countries, such as Sri Lanka, UNHCR is currently providing humanitarian assistance to internally displaced people. Issues such as the special problem of internally displaced persons and the limitations of the UN system, in this regard, need greater attention and action.
6. The promise of United Nations Security Council Resolution 688 can only be realized if the principles that it establishes are not applied selectively.
7. The right to humanitarian assistance is universal and a cease-fire is not considered to be a necessary precondition for the delivery of such aid. Furthermore, such assistance can still have a peacebuilding potential.

II. Preparation

8. The successful achievement of a humanitarian cease-fire is related to the combatants' confidence in the salience, reliability, and trustworthiness of the agency or agencies attempting to negotiate and implement that cease-fire.

9. Education is another critical part of the humanitarian cease-fire process and must proceed on several fronts: combatants, donors, and the international community must be educated about their obligations under international law; the public at large must be educated about the conditions of children in war zones in an effort to mobilize public opinion; and peace education, as part of the peacebuilding process, must be encouraged in war zones. Distance education of children, by means such as radio teaching or correspondence courses, can complement standard education and is an alternative when other means are not available. Training of community health care workers can strengthen the outcome of these initiatives.

10. The concept of devoting radio time, "Hours of Peace," could be used to promote peace by establishing a moral climate and cultivating attitudes conducive to peace.

11. In some conflict zones, peace education may be necessary prior to the implementation of humanitarian cease-fires. It is proposed that missions be undertaken to investigate the possibility of establishing education for peace programs in such cases, aimed at setting the stage for subsequent peacebuilding measures.

12. International public opinion is crucial in motivating governments both to undertake special measures to protect children and to oppose measures that work to the detriment of their well being.

13. Careful attention must be paid to the technical obstacles faced by the combatants that may work against their ability to comply

effectively with the terms of the cease- fire. These obstacles may include matters such as the command and control capacity of the combatants affecting their ability to police and implement their role in the cease-fire. A greater measure of attention needs to be provided to monitor and ensure the safe and successful delivery of aid under all circumstances.

14. Attention must be focused on identifying the motivations for combatants to participate in a humanitarian cease-fire; considerations such as an enhanced local or international image; genuine humanitarian concerns on the part of the combatants; and their desire for confidence building measures to advance the peace process. We are moving toward fundamental principles with respect to the value and dignity of human life shared by all groups, even those involved in armed conflict. It is to these values that appeals for humanitarian and peacemaking goals must be addressed.

III. Involvement

15. When delivering aid during a humanitarian cease-fire and otherwise, it is critical that international agencies and donor governments include indigenous national and local NGOs and grassroots and peoples' organizations in the process. This will, among other things, strengthen their capacities to continue contributing to the peacebuilding process.
16. The voices of the affected people and communities must be brought into the peacemaking process. In particular, the perspectives of women and children are needed in promoting humanitarian measures and children's needs in war-torn areas.
17. Attention and study must be given to the role of external actors (states and mediators) including the influence they might be able to use to ensure the successful negotiation of a humanitarian cease-fire. Their potential negative influence on the process must

also be borne in mind. We must also be vigilant in ensuring that humanitarian cease-fires are not exploited for partisan purposes.

18. International non-governmental organizations have been important contributors to the facilitation of humanitarian cease-fires. Their unique capacity for neutrality and ability to act without the constraints of governments and official agencies may be helpful.

IV. Follow-up

(A) Of a cease-fire:

19. Opportunities must be pursued so that the humanitarian measures undertaken during a cease-fire are extended, where possible, into rehabilitative and reconstructive measures. The process of a cease-fire must not take place in a socio-economic vacuum.

20. Recognizing that all peoples have a fundamental right to humanitarian assistance, speedy and creative ways must be found to resolve the deadlock with Iraq so that adequate funds can be made available to meet the survival needs of all Iraqi people in all parts of the country without prejudice. Within the framework of resolution 702 and 706, the United Nations should insist on a rigourous system to monitor distribution of food and medicine to all people of Iraq.

(B) Of this conference:

21. The concept of humanitarian cease-fires would benefit from the development of an international network for days of peace that would distribute information through worldwide affiliates.

22. The creation is recommended of an impartial body which does not have the responsibility to act, but has the responsibility to identify and evaluate situations of conflict, and to inform the international community where international intervention for the purposes of humanitarian assistance may be warranted.

23. The governments of the world should be challenged to devote substantial resources each year to a child survival fund. This money should be used to address survival of children in war torn areas.
24. Humanitarian cease-fires take on increasing urgency in a time when conventional war is made more lethal by the wide availability of advanced weapons. At the same time, in this period of rapid international change, there are greater opportunities for advancing this concept.
25. This conference on humanitarian cease-fires must be the beginning of a process of further conferences on the issue, including regional conferences and those which address issues in the broader context of peacebuilding and peacemaking.

ENDNOTES

* Unless otherwise noted, quotations are taken from conference proceedings or interviews.

Part One: Youth: The First Victims

1. Sivard, Ruth Leger. *World Military and Social Expenditures* 1991. Washington: World Priorities, 1991. p.20.
2. Davies, Peter. *Human Rights*. London: Routledge, 1988. p.42.
3. Ressler, Everett, Neil Boothby, and Daniel Steinbock. *Unaccompanied Children*. New York: Oxford University Press, 1988. p.149.
4. Garbarino, James, K. Kostelny, and N. Dubrow. *No Place to Be a Child*. Toronto: Lexington Books, 1991. p.150.
5. Perry, Thomas L. (ed). *Peacemaking in the 1990s*. Vancouver: Gordon Soules Book Publishers Ltd., 1990. p.143.
6. *UNICEF Annual Report 1991*. New York: United Nations, p.3.
7. Author's interview with Dr. Ed Ragan, Ottawa.
8. *First Call for Children*. United Nations Children's Fund, New York: United Nations, 1990. p.20.
9. Hay, Robin. *Humanitarian Ceasefires: An Examination of Their Potential Contribution to the Resolution of Conflict*. Ottawa: Canadian Institute for International Peace and Security, 1990. p.13.

Part Two: Some Success Stories

1. Gilmour, David. *Lebanon: The Fractured Country*. London: Sphere Books Ltd., 1984. p.x.
2. Minear, Larry. *A Critical Review of Operation Lifeline Sudan*. Washington: Refugee Policy Group, 1990. p.26.
3. Al-Khalil, Samir. "Iraq and Its Future." *The New York Review of Books,* March 18, 1991. p.10.

Part Three: War-torn World

1. *Report of the Parliamentary Delegation to Ethiopia and Sudan*. Ottawa: House of Commons, January 1991. p.26.
2. Finnegan, William. "A Reporter at Large, The Emergency-II." *The New Yorker,* May 29, 1989. p. 73.

3. Finnegan, William. "A Report at Large, The Emergency - I." *The New Yorker*, May 22, 1989. p.57.
4. *SARDC Destabilization Update No.9.* Harare, Zimbabwe: Southern Africa Research and Documentation Centre, August 15, 1991. p.4.
5. Ahlstrom, Christer. *Casualties of Conflict.* Uppsala University, Sweden, 1991. p.19.
6. Finnegan, William. "A Reporter at Large, The Emergency - II" *The New Yorker*, May 29, 1989. p. 48.
7. Vokey, Richard. "The Philippines: Democracy's Struggle to Survive." *Issues* Vol. 3, No. 6, Fall 1989. Vancouver: Asia Pacific Foundation of Canada. p. 4.
8. Garcia, Ed. *Dawn Over Darkness: Paths to Peace in the Philippines.* Quezon City: Claretian Publications, 1989. p.70.
9. Lernoux, Penny. "A Society Torn Apart by Violence." *The Nation*, Nov. 7, 1987. p. 512.

Part Four: Growing Up Peaceful

1. Eban, Abba. *The New Diplomacy.* New York: Random House, 1983. p. 265.
2. Hoffmann, Stanley. "Delusions of World Order." *The New York Review of Books*, April 9, 1992. p.40.
3. Hay, John. "Yugoslavia crisis helps UN appreciate 'preventive diplomacy.' " *Ottawa Citizen*, Nov. 27, 1991.
4. Pérez de Cuellar, Javier. *Report of the Secretary-General on the Work of the Organization*, New York: United Nations, 1991. p. 12.
5. Ibid, p.13.
6. Last draft of Conference Statement. p.4.
7. Conference Statement. 1991. p. 4.
8. Boutros-Ghali, Boutros. *Report of the Secretary-General: An Agenda for Peace.* New York: United Nations, June 17, 1992.
9. "New Rules for Tangled Wars." *The Economist*, Oct. 18, 1986. p. 50.
10. Ahlstrom, Christer. *Casualties of Conflict.* Uppsala University, Sweden, 1991.
11. *First Call for Children.* United Nations Children's Fund, New York: United Nations, 1990. p. 57.
12. "Brief to the International Commission on Human Rights," Geneva, Defence for Children International. 1992.
13. Hossie, Linda. "UN set to overhaul ineffective disaster-relief system." *The Globe and Mail.* Dec. 19, 1991.
14. "Strengthening of the Coordination of Humanitarian Emergency Assistance of the United Nations." UN General Assembly, December 18, 1991. p. 8.

ENDNOTES

15. Conference Statement. p. 7.
16. Urquhart, Brian. "Who Can Stop Civil Wars?" *The New York Times*, Dec. 29, 1991.
17. Gordon, Nancy. "The Right Move at Last." *Ottawa Citizen*, Dec. 7 1992.
18. Minear, Larry. *A Critical Review of Operation Lifeline Sudan*. Washington: Refugee Policy Group, 1990. p. 14.
19. Hay, Robin. *Humanitarian Ceasefires*. Ottawa: CIIPS, 1990. p.29.
20. Thier, J. Alexander. *A First Step Toward Peace: The Humanitarian Confidence-Building Measure*. Honours Thesis. Brown University, April 1992.
21. Miller, Robert, ed. *Aid as Peacemaker*. Ottawa: Carleton University Press, 1992. p. 172.

BIBLIOGRAPHY

Youth: The First Victims

The Problem of War

Davies, Peter (ed). *Human Rights*. Routledge, London. (1988).

Garbarino, James, K.Kostelny and N.Dubrow. *No Place To Be a Child*. Lexington Books, Toronto. (1991).

Perry, Thomas L. (ed). *Peacemaking in the 1990s*. Gordon Soules Book Publishers Ltd., Vancouver (1990).

Ressler, Everett M., Neil Boothby and Daniel Steinbock. *Unaccompanied Children*. Oxford University Press, New York. (1988).

Rosenblatt, Roger. *Children of War*. Anchor Books, New York. (1984).

Sivard, Ruth Leger. *World Military and Social Expenditures* 1991. World Priorities, Washington.

A New Era of Opportunities

Hay, Robin. *Humanitarian Ceasefires: An Examination of Their Potential Contribution to the Resolution of Conflict*. Canadian Institute for International Peace and Security. (1990).

Cease-fires: Some Success Stories

El Salvador

LaFeber, Walter. *Inevitable Revolutions*. W.W.Norton & Company, New York. (1983).

North, Liisa. *Bitter Grounds: Roots of Revolt in El Salvador*. Between the Lines, Toronto. (1985).

Lebanon

Giannou, Dr. Chris. *Besieged*. Key Porter Books, Toronto. (1990).

Gilmour, David. *Lebanon: The Fractured Country*. Sphere Books Ltd., London. (1984).

Sudan

Bonner, Raymond. "Famine." *The New Yorker*, Mar.13, 1989.

Minear, Larry. *Humanitarianism Under Siege*. The Red Sea Press Inc., Trenton, N.J. (1991).

Minear, Larry. *A Critical Review of Operation Lifeline Sudan*. Refugee Policy Group, Washington. (1990).

Iraq, Iran, and Kuwait

Al-Khalil, Samir. *Republic of Fear*. Pantheon Books, New York. (1990).

Chaliand, Gerard (ed). *People Without a Country*. Zed Press, London. (1980).

War-torn World: The Troubled Search for Peace

Horn of Africa: Ethiopia/Eritrea
Lefort, Rene. *Ethiopia: An Heretical Revolution?* Zed Press, London. (1981).

Somalia
Gordon, Nancy. "The Right Move at Last." *Ottawa Citizen*, Dec. 7, 1992.

Watson, Paul. "Children: Sacrificed on the Altar of War." *Toronto Star*, Feb.-March, 1992.

Wells, Rick. "Shell-Shocked: Somalia." *Focus on Africa*, March, 1992.

Mozambique
Finnegan, William. "A Reporter at Large: The Emergency – Mozambique — I & II." *The New Yorker*, May 22 and May 29,1989.

Moorcraft, Paul. "Mozambique's Long Civil War-Renamo." *International Defense Review*, Oct. 1987.

Sri Lanka
Phadnis, Urmila. *Ethnic Conflict in Sri Lanka*. Gandhi Peace Foundation, New Delhi. (1984).

Spaeth, Anthony. "Inventing an Ethnic Rivalry." *Harper's Magazine*, November, 1991.

Burma/Myanmar
Aung San, Suu Kyi. *Freedom From Fear*. Penguin Books, London, (1991).

Maung, Maung. *Burma and General Ne Win*. Asia Publishing House, Bombay. (1969).

The Philippines
Bonner, Raymond. *Waltzing with a Dictator*. Vintage Books, New York. (1988).

Garcia, Ed. *A Distant Peace*. National Book Store Inc., Manila. (1991).

Poole, Fred and Vanzi, Max. *Revolution in the Philippines*. McGraw-Hill Book Co., New York. (1984).

Colombia
Collett, Merrill. "The Myth of the Narco-Guerrillas." *The Nation*, Aug.13, 1988.

Lernoux, Penny. *Cry of the People*. Doubleday & Company Inc., New York. (1980).

Lernoux, Penny. "A Society Torn Apart by Violence." *The Nation*, Nov. 7, 1987.

Sanders, Thomas G. *Colombia, Betancur, and the Challenge of 1984*. Universities Field Staff International Inc., Hanover, N.H. (1984).

Yugoslavia

Battiata, Mary. "The Littlest Victims in the Land of the Living Dead." *Washington Post Weekly,* Dec. 6, 1992.

Glenny, Misha. "The Massacre of Yugoslavia." *New York Review of Books,* Jan.30, 1992.

Scammell, Michael. "Yugoslavia: The Awakening" and "The New Yugoslavia." *New York Review of Books,* June 28 and July 19, 1990.

Growing Up Peaceful

The Limits of Sovereignty

Ahlstrom, Christer. *Casualties of Conflict. Report for the World Campaign for the Protection of Victims of War.* Department of Peace and Conflict Research. Uppsala University, Sweden. (1991).

Eban, Abba. *The New Diplomacy.* Random House, New York. (1983)

Hoffmann, Stanley. "Delusions of World Order." *New York Review of Books,* April 9, 1992.

Urquhart, Brian. "The United Nations and Its Discontents." *New York Review of Books,* Mar.15,1990.

The Right to Help

First Call for Children. United Nations Children's Fund. United Nations, New York. (1990).

Hay, Robin. *Civilian Aspects of United Nations Peacekeeping.* Canadian Institute for International Peace and Security, Ottawa, (1991).

Macpherson, Martin. "Child Soldiers." Report of Quaker Peace and Service, London. (1992).

Pérez de Cuellar, Javier. *Report of the Secretary-General on the Work of the Organization, 1991.* United Nations, New York. (1991).

Peacebuilding for Children: A Manifesto

Boutros-Ghali, Boutros. *Report of the Secretary-General. An Agenda for Peace.* United Nations, New York. (1992).

Miller, Robert, ed. *Aid as Peacemaker.* Carleton University Press, Ottawa. (1992).

Thier, J. Alexander. "A First Step Toward Peace: The Humanitarian Confidence-Building Measure." Honors Thesis, Brown University, April, 1992.

Yarrow,C.H.Mike. *Quaker Experiences in International Conciliation.* Yale University Press, London.(1978).

Conference Statement. "Humanitarian Ceasefires: Peacebuilding for Children." Centre for Days of Peace, Ottawa, 1991.

PRINTED IN CANADA